87
Sundays

JOHN BAXTER

PAGE PUBLISHING, INC.
New York, NY

First originally published by Page Publishing, Inc. 2017

ISBN 978-1-64138-243-4 (Paperback)
ISBN 978-1-64138-244-1 (Digital)

Printed in the United States of America

Foreword

When I began writing *87 Sundays*, I prayed a lot that God reveal more of himself to me.

This way I could give the reader a better picture of the beauty of Christ. God always had a way of showing up in his perfect timing. In so many ways, my prayers were answered. There is no greater peace than to lie down at night then to be visited by angels and even Jesus himself. I don't remember what I was doing on this particular day. But after my prayers and then lying down, I drifted into a peaceful state. And this is what happened:

I found myself in a little run-down shack, or perhaps it was a small rustic cabin. The more I think about it now, it was more like a shack. I stood at a kitchen sink peeling potatoes. Although the shack was very small, it was one large open area. It smelled of dank pine wood, and although it was rather dirty, it felt very homelike. I was very focused on a meal preparation. I didn't even know who I was preparing it for. I always loved to cook; it was like a form of art for me.

As I gazed into the empty living area, a light began to fill the room. Then suddenly out of the light stood what appeared to be Jesus and two men. Jesus stood in the center of the two men. I became very excited I wanted to rush toward him and begin worshipping him. At the same time, I was almost paralyzed with excitement and fear. He looked at me, I looked at him, and nothing was ever said. He already knew how I felt. I started to step around the side of the countertop to greet him and praise him! When all of a sudden he and the two men fled from the center of the room and vanished right through a wooden wall.

I stood there bewildered for a moment and then went to the center of the room where Jesus and the two men once stood. I thought to myself, "Where did he go?" Then all of a sudden there was a knock at the door, and a joy began to fill my heart that I couldn't describe in words. I just knew that it was Jesus! I danced my way through the living area over to the door. I felt like the giddiest little kid, yet I was the same thirty-two-year-old man. Then he knocked again. I reached for the doorknob, turning it slowly, and began opening the door. When the door had opened, I instantly fell to my knees, and a light began to fill the room. I was in the presence of the King of Glory. Suddenly I awakened I felt so serene and was mesmerized by what took place. Was this really a dream?

In retrospect of this dream, vision, or revelation, I was first reminded of the Gospel of John 10, Jesus the Good Shepard. Even though Jesus never spoke vocally, his presence and knock said it all! Just as in John 10:3 KJV: To him the porter openeth; and the sheep hear his voice: and he calleth his sheep by name and leadeth them out. John 10:7 goes on to say: Verily I say to you I am the door of the sheep.

And finally John 10:9: I am the door; by me if any man enter he shall be saved. Jesus is very real! When you truly seek him, you shall find him. It wasn't long after this I was blessed with an idea of baptism. This idea would probably receive scrutiny from the Church. I don't follow a path of legalism but of spiritualism led by the Holy Spirit. I am very passionate about scripture, particularly what it spoke of in Matthew 3. John the Baptist was preparing the way of the Lord by water baptisms unto repentance. In so many ways, I could relate to John the Baptist because I had dwelled in a desert my entire life.

The Holy Spirit revealed to me that this book would lead people to Christ, not only to follow him but to do his work here on earth until his return. Something that was also revealed to me starts with in the days of Noah. Noah warned the earth's inhabitants of the wrath to come and it would be destroyed by water. In those days, the world had become an utterly perverse place, and God doubted his creation. There were only eight survivors to create the future generations of mankind. God vowed that he would never destroy the world by water again. Jesus spoke that the desolation would be by fire, and how he wished it were already kindled some two thousand years ago.

The Lord revealed to me that our truest repentance comes by our tears. A flood of tears! It will not destroy you, although the pain may seem too much to bear. It is the purest form of living water. There are no lies in tears. If you can allow the walls around your heart to come crashing down, then allow the floodgates to open, each tear is carefully collected by an angel as a prayer and delivered before the Throne of God.

I assure you by the honesty and purity of your tears, Jesus will eventually come to your dwelling. Mine just so happened to be an old run-down shack; however, it felt more like home than anywhere I've ever been. It was filled by his immeasurable love, and I am certain that shack has now become a mansion. Jesus said, "In my Father's house, there are many mansions." I urge you to open your heart while reading this book. As your spirit awakens, be still and wait on the Lord. He will soon be knocking at your door.

Runnin' with the Devil

I was born in Xenia, Ohio, on Friday, thirteenth of April 1979; it happened to be a Good Friday. My Mom was a waitress; she would leave me alone with my biological father to go to work. She did her best in trying to support me. One incident that led up to her divorcing my father was that she came home and found him passed out intoxicated. I was alone in my playpen bleeding very badly from my hand. Apparently, my father gave me a glass peanut butter jar to play with, and I broke it. My mother finally ended her marriage to my father after discovering he was having an affair. She kicked him out, and he then left to Florida, where he was from. I never saw or heard from him until much later in my life.

My mother continued to be a waitress and, eventually, met another man who happened to be a short-order cook at the restaurant she worked at. They would eventually marry, and I would grow up to call this man Dad. My earliest memory was a memory of torture. We had moved to Texas, and I was about three, or maybe 3½ years old. We were taking a ship across the Gulf of Mexico to go see a doctor for my health condition. I remember my stepfather holding me over the edge of the ship and acting as though he were going to drop me over the edge. It was very traumatizing for me at that age.

The torment didn't stop there. When I was young, I was extremely terrified of witches. My parents were both drug addicts, and this is still something my mother refuses to admit. It was close to 1983, and my parents would get a kick out of luring me into my bedroom. They would turn off all the lights and then shove me into the closet while holding the door shut, saying, "There's witches in there, Johnny!"

I would scream as though it were the end of my life. I spent a lot of time alone in this room, what I thought was one of my better memories as a child would play a crucial role for the next thirty-one years of my life. I had a small '45 record player and a vinyl record of Van Halen's song "Runnin' with the Devil." I would play this song over and over and over. At the time, I didn't even know what it had meant. Music was my means of escape from the constant hostility I was forced to endure.

I remember taking some serious beatings as a child. I also remember waking up in my bed one morning completely naked not knowing at all how I got that way. I just remember feeling confused and dirty, so I rushed to find some clothes and put them on. My stepfather also used to take a lot of pictures of me naked; he would tell my mother it was a form of art. I don't have complete evidence that I was ever molested; it's something that still boggles my mind today. I do know that I was given alcohol at a very early age. And I was given enough to the point I was drunk and passed out in a plate of spaghetti.

When I was 4½ years old, my little sister was born; at this time in my life, we lived in Texas. I was very jealous of her because I saw all the attention and love that she got. Love and attention I got from my stepfather was very different. I don't think that my stepfather ever truly loved me. My little sister looked up to me though. I was her hero. But I would only push her away. She too would suffer from the abuse and hostility in our home. Everyone was a victim in my family. We moved back to Ohio. My stepfather was a musician, and one of his friends convinced him to move back and start a record label while building a recording studio. Music would become the most influential part of my life. Before my parents found a house, we stayed with my grandmother, my mother's mom. I had a bad habit of lying as a child. I lived in fear of my stepfather, so whenever I was confronted about something I did wrong, I would lie. I remember him becoming enraged one time about my lying; he took off his belt and then hit me in the face with it. The belt buckle busted my nose wide open. My grandmother came to my aid and cleaned me up.

She said, "Johnny, I won't let him hurt you anymore."

But it didn't stop there. My stepfather was a cocaine addict. There were times he wouldn't even come home, and I pray to God earnestly he would never come back. But he would, sometimes days later, and he would then beat my mom up.

One night I came out of my room to find my mother lying in a huge pool of blood from a pot that he had broken over her face. My mom and I would leave. I always was on my mom's side. I loved her so much and wanted to protect her in my adolescence but felt powerless. I would beg her not to go back, but she always would. Only to endure more suffering, then we all would suffer. I went to Dayton City Schools, and my elementary years were a blessing. Time continued progress; abuse, both physical and mental, continued to endure.

While one door would open, I would strive to enter it and feel so alone going through it. I didn't feel any support in anything I ever did. My mother would try; she would come to one baseball game, one young scholars' meeting, and due to my stepfather's selfishness, she would even sneak to buy me a pair of name-brand shoes so I wouldn't get teased at school. It hurt so very bad to see such a beautiful woman stay and to be treated the way she was.

I know now it was fear and the devil's influence ruling our home. I truly believed my stepfather to be a product of evil. But God being who he is and in complete control always seemed to make a way outside of my home for me. I started going to a middle school for the performing arts. I sang in the choir, excelling in visual arts for photography, and I loved to write. My grades were good up to this point despite the hostility in my home life. Eventually, I would start smoking cigarettes, lose interest in sports, and gain the interest of what everyone thought of me. I sought acceptance. I wanted an identity. I started to hang out with kids who had similar home lives, kids who came from a place of brokenness too. I just wanted to hang out with who I thought were my friends. I never wanted to go home. I would try to stay away as much as possible.

Anger started to really grow inside me about this time. I took my frustrations out on my siblings. I started to rebel, and it earned me some kind of attention; however, it always ended up in some form of abuse. I didn't know what love was; my opinion of it was so warped. I knew I truly despised my stepfather, yet somehow I loved him, looked up to him, and just wanted to be accepted by him. I longed for him to embrace me as his son, but it never happened. I came to a point in my early teenage years that I wasn't going to allow my stepfather to physically abuse my mother anymore.

I was upstairs one afternoon, and my stepfather had been remodeling my room. He had tools up there, and I overheard my mother screaming. I looked around the room and found a large drywall knife he was using. I grabbed it and slowly crept down the stairs. I had made up in my mind that I would kill him for hurting her. I opened the door to find him slinging my mother around trying to take her purse. I demanded that he let her go and showed him the knife. He wickedly laughed at me and drew back his fist, then punched me in the face, probably the hardest I have ever been hit in my life.

My mother rushed to me. I was dazed by the hit, so she grabbed me by the arm and ran with me out of the house. Once again we would go back; however, he would never physically harm my mother again. Shortly after that incident, my parents decided to get away and arranged for a white water rafting trip. My stepfather's mom would come to the house and watch us kids while they were gone. I took full advantage of this opportunity to stay gone and do what I wanted to do. I had an older friend who lived up the street from me, so on one afternoon, I went to hang out with him. He offered me a beer and was rolling up what appeared to be a cigarette. I drank the beer and asked for another then as he lit what I thought was a cigarette; a peculiar smell invaded the room. I then knew it was marijuana. He passed me the joint, so I tried it. Once the high began to kick in, I became very sick to the point of nausea and almost instantly paranoid. I didn't like it, but I did like the effects of alcohol; it made me feel a false sense of bravery.

I was just about to start high school, and from that point on, I decided I was going to do what I wanted, whenever I wanted. I started drinking alcohol very heavily. I also started experimenting with other drugs such as LSD, Xanax, and Vicodin. Under the influence of these mind-altering chemicals, my home life almost started to seem bearable. But the devil continued to dominate my home on Tuttle Avenue. I stopped caring; my little sister acted well beyond her age, much like a care-taking mother. My little brother didn't show any emotions; he would stare at the TV watching cartoons as the yelling, breaking, and slamming of things went on around him.

My mother started keeping a box of wine in the fridge at most times. My stepfather would stay in the basement getting high, making music, only to come up and vent his frustrations or to play Dad when my mother had become too overwhelmed.

By the time I started high school, I gave up on dreams and aspirations. All I wanted to do was party. I wanted to do drugs, fight, and have sex with just about any girl I could do it with, to feel a sense of security. I went to a high school in Dayton called Belmont. I literally would enter in through the front door then go right out the back door into the alley to hang out with all the derelict kids much like myself. We would get high all day long and do absolutely nothing. I would return to school just in time to catch the bus home then go listen to the preaching of my stepfather about how I needed to live my life and just how messed up I really was. My stepfather was a very intelligent man; he was full of knowledge, but he lacked wisdom. I truly believed he just enjoyed hearing himself talk just to make others feel stupid. It wasn't long after being in high school that I lost my scholarship. I was hanging out in the ghettos of Dayton, Ohio, with what most people would call lowlifes. I started constantly getting suspended from school, so I eventually dropped out.

I was about sixteen or seventeen, and I tried cocaine for the very first time. It grabbed ahold of me unlike any other drug I had done. It gave me a false sense of power and purpose. It became the drug that would control my life for the next eleven years. God was still trying to make a way for me in the midst of my self-inflicted madness.

My neighbor got me a job doing heating and air. I was seventeen years old. I really loved this job. I worked with a lot of older guys whom I looked up to. However, they all drank and did drugs. I yearned for a father figure. I got my license, and my mother convinced my stepfather into helping me by a car to commute back and forth to work. I would get paid on a Friday, then go over to some guy's house in the ghetto and spend every single dime I had on cocaine and alcohol. After all my money was gone and the sun had risen, I would go back to my parents' home and sleep into oblivion.

I started falling into a deep, dark depression. My parents were fed up, so they kicked me out of the house. I went and stayed with a girl much older than myself who worked in a go-go bar as an exotic dancer. I would use her up to drink lethal amounts of alcohol while snorting cocaine. This is where my legal trouble began. Somehow I managed to keep a clean record as a juvenile. However, at the age of eighteen, I left a party highly intoxicated. I drove across town and was pulled over. I received a DUI, but by the grace of God, I didn't hurt anyone or myself. After spending the weekend in jail, I thought to myself that wasn't so bad, but not even a month later, I was convicted for my second DUI. I had no respect for authority, but I was taught a hard lesson by doing thirty days in the county jail.

After I was released, I continued to use cocaine and alcohol. I started staying with some childhood acquaintances who just so happened to sell drugs.

One evening they had eaten a lot of Xanax and misplaced their drugs. I knew where they were and seized the opportunity to rob them for a large amount of cocaine. They soon would find out that it was me who did it, then began making threats toward my life and the lives of my family members.

This is where a level of my insanity began to really progress. I bought a shotgun from a guy at the end of my street, sawed off the barrel and the handle, then waited on the front porch to see if they would show up. I was scared, paranoid, and felt the need to protect my family. I would hide the shotgun on the side of the garage just as the sun would come up. I didn't even consider the dangers of my little brother or sister ever finding it. My stepfather would soon discover the shotgun and destroyed it.

My parents had become fed up with my behaviors and wanted me to leave, I had nowhere to go, so my mother was able to locate my biological father. My mother always told me growing up that he was an animal and I would be very disappointed to meet him.

When I was angry at my parents I always dreamed and hoped that he would be a great guy maybe even become my hero. So I left for Florida to meet him. When I arrived in Florida I met an angry man who claimed to be a recovering alcoholic. He lived with his mother, my grandmother was a very sweet and loving woman but was always wasted on nerve pills. My biological father never attended a meeting of recovery nor did he ever talk about God. He was absolutely a miserable man. The only time that I ever saw him happy was while we were fishing off of the pier in Clearwater Florida. It wasn't long after me being in Florida that my biological father wanted me gone, I felt rejected yet once again. According to him I was a financial burden and to tell the truth I think he was rather scared of me. I genuinely just wanted to know the man who had contributed to creating me. I wasn't there to judge him. I left feeling unwanted much like I felt my entire life.

I was able to get a job in Florida and was looking for a place but continued to use drugs and alcohol. One evening I was drinking with a cousin, when his grandfather came out of the house and started a conversation with us. He said to me that I was basically a miracle, I asked him how so? He then proceeded to tell me a story of how my biological father had severely beat my mother while she was pregnant with me. It was very graphic and instantly I became enraged. I went to my grandmother's house she answered the door, I saw my biological father standing about thirteen feet from the doorway and I yelled in at him.

I called him outside, saying, "You may have contributed to bringing me into this world, but I'm here to take you out!" He wouldn't come out of the house and my grandmother begged me to stop then started crying, so I left. The longing to know him turned out to be one of the biggest disappointments in my life. My mother was absolutely right about him.

I stayed in Florida for a little while longer basically bouncing from house to house on couch to couch. I eventually returned back to Dayton, Ohio, in the summer of 1999. I was twenty years old, when I returned home. I discovered my mother had left and was divorcing my stepfather, I was very relieved when at the same time I sympathized for him, because it crippled him mentally. And as this all was taking place I began to form a resentment against my mother, for waiting until I was grown and gone to finally leave him.

Now I never considered myself a ladies man actually I was quite insecure, but being that music was such a huge part of my life it allowed me to feel a sense of importance. The flip side to that coin was it also allowed me to engage in the fast lifestyle of sex, drugs, and rock 'n' roll. In any other area of my life I felt defeated but when I was on stage I was someone else, I felt complete. I met a beautiful woman who would try to stay with me off and on for five years.

Around this time I also met who would become my best friend, a friend to this day who still stands by my side. When things would go south between my girlfriend and I, I would go stay at my best friend's house. Truth be told, I manipulated both situations to my advantage, because I didn't want to be held accountable to anyone. I would cheat on my then girlfriend who was an amazing woman that was worthy of marrying. I, however, could not add up.

My addiction in creation with the devil at my heels continued to tear down anything and everyone around me. I would continue to drink alcohol and use cocaine for days on end. I couldn't keep a job, I lived off of women and used other people. I was in and out of jail for drinking, violence, and violating the terms of probation that I was always on. I was physically abusive to my girlfriend, I would break things, steal money and not feel the least bit sorry about anything I had done. I crushed this woman and I really didn't even care. Throughout the years she put up with a lot and she eventually left me for another man. So I then ran to my best friend's home in whom I was so codependent toward. My best friend was getting ready to move to Virginia to live with her family. I was in some legal trouble and rather than dealing with the consequences I chose to flee to Virginia and follow after her. I stayed in Virginia for a short amount of time and soon found a band that was looking for a vocalist in Winston Salem North Carolina.

That experience was short-lived and I came back to Dayton, Ohio, and was sentenced to six months in jail. After I was released I stayed with my mother who had her own apartment at the time. My mother was a bartender and got me a job at the tavern she worked at. This allowed me to drink all the alcohol I wanted and do all the cocaine that I could mentally handle. My boss would give me cocaine just so I would show up for work. I continued to use music for my selfish gain. I found a band looking for a singer in Middletown Ohio, the band was Edge of Life. They were a group of very professional musicians and after the auditioning process I was selected to be there vocalist. I was so excited that I went to my mother's work one night and was drinking a lot of alcohol with off-duty Dayton police officers. It was closing time and I helped my mom close up the bar. My mother had been drinking too and we both had become very intoxicated.

We got to her vehicle I had a CD of my audition with Edge of Life. I put it in the CD player and said something offensive to my mother, she immediately reached over and punched me in the face. In that moment I blacked out and I bounced my mother's face off of the steering wheel in her car. I got out of the car in below zero weather. She sped off drunk and after I realized what I had done, I stood there hating myself, I truly had become the animal that I despised. I went to Middletown, my mother pressed charges and I was convicted of my first domestic violence. I was so ashamed of what I had done to my mother.

I tried to block it out with the music, drugs, and women but I was stuck in this continuous grip of evil. The band started recording a CD in Nashville, Tennessee. We even had a Grammy award-winning producer supporting us. I developed the hope that I was going to make it in the music industry.

While in Nashville, I was in my hotel room getting ready to go record vocal tracks. I was getting ready to leave then suddenly the telephone rang. It was my ex-girlfriend and she had my mother on a three-way call. My mother was crying and said that my little sister had been missing after my stepfather kicked her out of the house. I had no idea that my little sister had went missing, I was completely disconnected from my family. My mother continued to tell me that my little sister was arrested for prostitution of crack cocaine. My heart sank. I wasn't there to protect her and as a big brother I always wanted to protect her. Even though I wasn't a good brother, but I'll be damned if I would let anyone else hurt her.

I immediately fell to my knees after getting off of the phone. God has always been very pertinent in different areas of my life, up to this point I hadn't talked to God in a very long time. I prayed from my heart and in tears that God would protect her, comfort her, and deliver her from the evil that she would suffer while using drugs. I am forced to live with the guilt of getting high with my little sister although I had never smoked crack cocaine I remember a time where I had a plate full of cocaine and was using it in my little sister's bedroom. She came into the room and discovered what I was doing, smacked me across the face and then smacked the plate out of my hand. She had never used drugs, and it wasn't long after, she was using them. In some strange way, I grew close to my sister by using drugs with her; we would have long emotional conversations about our childhood and our dreams. She always maintained such a beautiful spirit about her.

I loved my little sister so much I would do anything to have a chance to take back those years. After my little sister was released from jail she was placed on probation and went to stay at my step-father's. She had fines and court costs to pay so my mother thought she would help by letting her work at the bar. I didn't like this at all! I was fearful of my little sister being around alcohol, drinking it and then going back to smoking crack. I know for me whenever I drank alcohol, it was like I was holding the hand of the devil as he was leading me on the chase to find cocaine.

One night after my little sister was released from jail I was over at my ex-girlfriend's house with my little brother. We were just about to watch a movie and the telephone rang. It was my mother who was calling from a bar with my little sister. I was angry but withheld how I felt. My mother asked me if I wanted to join them, I said no and in the background I could hear my little sister laughing. I got off of the phone in hopes of having an enjoyable evening with my little brother. I couldn't help but to keep thinking about my mother and my little sister, but I eventually fell asleep on the couch.

At 4:30 a.m. on July 31, 2004, the telephone rang. My ex-girl-friend answered the phone, it was my stepfather's new wife. My ex handed me the phone, and my stepfather's wife proceeded to tell me that my mother was involved in a car accident, and that my little sister had died in it. There is not a word within this world that I could ever associate with how I felt. As the funeral processions began it just didn't seem real to me. To me everyone seemed insincere about their condolences, most of the people at my sister's funeral I hadn't seen in ages. I was angry that they were nowhere around during the times we had went through all that we did.

I thought my little sister was severely cheated of her life, she was only twenty years old. Everyone would say I'm so sorry for your loss, but I never felt any sense of compassion from them. I was crushed. I turned my back on my mother. I wanted to blame her. And the person I actually felt compassion for was my stepfather, even after all he put us through. I've never really been one to hold a grudge, I still care for my stepfather. My whole family blamed my mother for the death of my little sister. Her very own family disowned her, I can only imagine how that must of made her feel.

After the death of my little sister, I told myself that I wasn't going to drink or use drugs. I became driven to arrange a music benefit to cover her funeral expenses. I arranged for eleven bands to play at an all-day event. I was going to take the proceeds and donate a portion of it toward drinking and driving awareness. After the money was collected my then stepfather's wife gave me a manila envelope full of money. She said to do what I saw fit with the money. I took the benefit money and got a tribute in tattoos of my sister. By the time I ended up back in Middletown Ohio, I had little support and comfort from my band mates and other people. We were getting ready to release our full-length CD *State of Mind*. I did manage to stay away from drinking and drugging only for a little while. But on those nights when I was completely alone, the pain and the thoughts of my little sister, my mother, and my family were almost unbearable. I felt so hopeless, I wanted to help my mother because her pain, was always my pain, no matter what it was. Feelings started to come out that were completely foreign to me, I never had any experience with grief. The devil would use this opportunity to push me to the edge, I then started smoking crack cocaine.

I wanted to see for myself, what exactly it was, that grabbed ahold of my little sister. I missed her so much and as I continued to fall into the depths of a living hell, I began telling myself that my little sister was in hell. I became delusional and I told myself that I was going to go to hell and would rescue her. I eventually lost the ambition to make music, I wanted out of my life. I attempted suicide, I slit my wrists, and violently cried as I bled while holding a picture of my little sister. I was completely out of my mind, due to all the drugs and alcohol I had been using. I stayed up for days smoking crack, drinking, and I stayed delusional, paranoid. I would look out of the windows of the house and thought I saw people staring at me, and they were crying for what I was doing to myself. My wrists bled to the point that I went into the kitchen and passed out in the floor, While awake, I couldn't look at myself in the mirror. I hadn't bathed, I hadn't eaten, and everywhere in the house were empty beer bottles.

My band mates eventually kicked me out of the band. I went back to Dayton, Ohio, and about this time my best friend had moved back from Virginia. She knew I had become a mess, but she would take me in, because I had no one and nowhere to go. I continued to smoke crack, I would steal from her, her son, lie, and cheat everyone around me. I was so angry at life, but couldn't admit the defeat of my human power against the influences of drugs and alcohol. I knew what and who I needed, I just wouldn't surrender to him. I continued to be in and out of jail. I remember the different volunteers coming in to preach the word of God, but I would just walk away. I didn't feel worthy of God's love, and the devil had kept me blind to it. I thought people who found God in jail were hypocrites.

Whenever I was released from jail, somehow I always managed to receive probation after doing thirty days here, or six months there. My mother would try to help me from time to time, I would have short periods of doing good, then eventually would sabotage everything I was working toward. I would harm and tear down anyone who came into my life, or tried to get close to me. After they got there feel of my pain, they wouldn't stay around long. I remained promiscuous, I would sleep with multiple women just to try to feel better about myself. I wanted to feel security but it just wasn't possible. I used everyone to get what I wanted, only to use drugs every day, all day. I had become the entertainment for demons. I was so ashamed of myself, but I just couldn't stop.

Life had become so overwhelming, I would try to get clean and sober but I couldn't handle life on its own terms. In my delusional way of thinking, I came up with the idea that if I had my own family and a child, things would get better for me. I met a woman that moved in across the street from my best friend's house. I had become desperate, and in the beginning she said everything I thought I needed to hear. Our relationship was founded by the use of drugs. It wasn't long after being with her we were fighting, and neglecting the needs of her other children. Even though she already had three kids, she too entertained the idea of wanting another baby.

I was twenty-eight years old at this time, one evening after using drugs and drinking I discovered her having a conversation with her ex-boyfriend. He had just gotten out of prison, I became enraged and assaulted her. I went to jail, and then later got out once again being on probation. I would discover shortly thereafter she was pregnant. We would try to work things out and began looking for a house. I found a job, yet struggled to stay clean and sober. I felt excited about wanting to be a Dad, even though I wasn't ready to be one. The company I worked for had a lot of other employees who also liked to party. One day I injured my back at work. The devil would use this to his advantage, my addict mind would say, "Johnny your hurt, you should eat some pain pills." So I relapsed. I began spending a lot of money to support my pill habit. I struggled to pay bills and meet the expectations as a head of household only to feed my addiction.

One morning on a job, a fellow coworker said, "Johnny, why do you waste so much money on those pills?" He then said, "I've got something that's much cheaper but more effective." After work I followed him over to his house, I watched as he pulled out two syringes and a small bag of tan color. He emptied the contents of the bag into a spoon, then used the syringe to squirt water on top of the powder. The drug was heroin. He lit a flame under the spoon, and it began to boil.

Finally he drew the tan liquid into the syringe and then said, "You'll love this."

Part of me was in fear of trying this, but the addict part of me chose differently. I took the needle into my arm, and as he pressed the plunge, it was a matter of seconds before the high kicked in. It was like the warmest comforting wave crashing all around me. Instantly all my cares toward life had dissipated. Heroin had become my drug of choice. Little did I know how strong this drug would grab ahold of me. I tried to hide my drug use as problems continued to escalate at home. My soon-to-be baby's mother eventually found out what I was doing, and then kicked me out of our home.

One afternoon I showed up at the house after nearly dying from an overdose while at a friend's. I knew that I desperately needed to make some changes, and I only wanted to talk with my soon-to-be baby's mother. She didn't want to hear what I had to say, and told me to leave. I still continued trying to reason with her, she then picked up the phone, locked herself in the bedroom and dialed 911. I unplugged the phone from the wall, but soon the police would show up. I was arrested for a verbal domestic violence and a felony in the fourth degree for disruption of public services. After all the court proceedings had taken place, I was ordered to go into a residential drug treatment facility. I completed a twenty-eight-day program and then rode what most people new to recovery would call the Pink Cloud. The problem with riding the pink cloud is that it usually vanishes rather quickly. Especially if a spiritual awakening hasn't occurred. I went to treatment for other people, not myself.

On New Year's Day of 2009, I went to my old home to visit with my soon-to-be baby's mother. She was just a little over eight months pregnant, and once again we would try to work things out for the sake of our child. I was able to witness the birth of my little girl, it was the most beautiful experience I could ever have. It was as though I had stepped into heaven and God had personally delivered to me one of his most precious Angels. As she opened her eyes, I was the very first thing she saw. For the very first time in my life I felt needed, and I truly had learned what love is. I battled to stay clean and sober, I went to meetings and became part of the Fellowship of Narcotics Anonymous. I got a sponsor and put forth a valiant effort toward being a good father and a provider.

I wanted to change, I wanted to feel whole, but I was still missing something and someone. The only one who could fill this void was God. I couldn't feel God in my prayers, I know now that it was because I hadn't been released from my bondage. And even though I couldn't feel him, he was always there, he was there all along. I'm the one who refused to acknowledge his presence. I was still running with the devil. I got to the third step out of the twelve and problems began to really show up for me. My daughter was about five or six months old. My daughter's mother and I both took jobs waiting tables at a newly opened restaurant. I stopped going to meetings and calling my sponsor, it wasn't long after that I started using heroin again. But this time it would bring me crashing to my knees.

One evening I ended up manipulating my daughter's mother into using heroin with me. I watched it grab ahold of her instantly as well. My feelings became numb toward my daughter. I knew that I loved her, but I always chose drugs over her. I felt so much guilt because I desperately wanted to be the dad she deserved but I just couldn't stop using drugs. As a result of my heroin use, I would overdose on many occasions. The devil was trying to take me out. For whatever reason, God wouldn't allow it. My daughter's mother would once again grow tired of me. I knew that she truly didn't love me, but I was addicted to dysfunctional relationships. She started seeing a guy at the restaurant we both worked at. When I found out, not only did it hurt but I became enraged. Here I was not only addicted to drugs but a woman who was the absolute worst for me. I went to our home even after she told me, she didn't want me there.

Of course I was drunk and high on heroin. She was asleep, so I picked up her phone and discovered a text message from the guy she became involved with. It read that she loved him. I was so jealous and angry that I woke her up by slapping her across the face. I was yelling as she called the police. While she was on the phone with them I kept saying, "Please don't do this to me!" I then went to the crib where my daughter lay, picked her up and held her in my arms. My little girl was so frightened. After kissing my daughter and saying, "I love you, one day you will know the truth," I then fled the house. I remember crying as I thought about her innocent little frightened face. I was already on intense probation for the domestic violence and the disruption of public services, the very next day I was arrested. This time I was arrested for another domestic violence that was a felony of the third degree.

While in the County jail I called my sponsor who I hadn't spoken to in months. I was withdrawing from heroin and was beating myself up mentally, about how long I would go to prison. I asked my sponsor to call my daughter's mother and ask her if she was going to press charges. I hung up the phone, then called my sponsor back about an hour later. He told me she was going to testify before the grand jury. I hung up the phone, and made my way up the stairs toward my cell. I told God, "This is it!" I took a sheet off of the mattress, then tied it around my neck, I then tied it to the upper bunk and hung myself. I passed out to the point that I was actually hanging from the bunk by all the weight from my body. As I was dying, I felt myself leaving my body.

My experience wasn't pleasant and it seemed that the devil would have his way. Another inmate just happened to be walking by my cell and looked inside of the window from the door. He yelled for the officer on duty. I was rushed to the hospital and was brought back to life by a defibrillator. After finally coming to at the hospital the nurse had asked me if I knew what happened. All I knew was, I was handcuffed to a gurney. I was given Percocet due to having bit a hole in my lip, I also severely damaged my throat.

After a few days in the hospital I was then transported back to the County jail. I was then sentenced to prison for a term of seven months. I didn't use any drugs while in prison, I also kept the attitude that I wouldn't become some Holy Roller hypocrite. I did nothing to better myself but the time had come for my release on February 6, 2010. My daughter would be turning one on February 9. I told myself while I was incarcerated that I was going to buy her all these wonderful gifts and I had painted a picture of something that I still wasn't ready to be. I was at the bus station, my anxiety was so intense and the devil was saying, "Let's go for a run!"

I had gotten a little over one hundred dollars for what is called gate pay. So I purchased my bus ticket, walked to the carryout down the street, purchased some alcohol and cigarettes. It wasn't long before I would become intoxicated. Having been inebriated, I approached the first person whom I thought would be a drug dealer. Sure enough my suspicions were correct. I bought some crack cocaine, then made my way to smoke it behind a church. After it was all gone, I went back to the bus station and saw a man lying in the floor waiting for his bus. He looked very familiar to me. It would turn out that I knew him, and that he was someone I used to shoot dope with. It goes without saying, I had a needle in my arm within an hour of having gotten out of prison.

I was running with the devil once again, but this time I was sprinting. I guess I really was on a journey to hell. I spent all my money, I missed my bus back to Dayton, while my mom was waiting with my daughter. I would sabotage a beautiful thing once again. I finally made it back to Dayton. I had my mom stop and purchase some alcohol then drank it with her. I spent a few days with my daughter, then seventeen days later I was back in jail. The judge would show me mercy, and once again I was sent into treatment. I didn't want to be there, and everyone knew it. I continued to throw myself a pity party. I did complete treatment, and it was only a short amount of time before I was snorting cocaine and drinking.

I missed my daughter terribly. I wasn't allowed to see her, but why should I be? I didn't deserve to be a father, I knew why and I shouldn't be allowed to destroy her innocent life, the torment of missing her continued to take me deeper and deeper. I felt as though I was chained in darkness. Mentally, physically, and spiritually. My daughter's mother had taken a restraining order out on me, one evening in a drunken stupor I decided to call her. She called the police then contacted my probation officer. I wasn't going to go back to jail, so I went on the run. I would use my vocal abilities, or at least what was left of it to join a band in Nashville Tennessee. I found a job as a cook, but wherever I went my addiction was sure to follow.

I didn't have any luck finding heroin, but I did find OxyContin and began shooting it. I desperately tried to erase everything and everyone from my mind, but it just wasn't possible.

I did my best to try and hide my dark secrets from my band mates. Until one day my guitarist would discover a needle and a spoon in my dirty laundry. My time had run out in Nashville, and I had no choice but to return to Dayton, Ohio, to face my consequences. While briefly staying at my mother's, one morning the phone rang and it was my daughter's grandmother. She proceeded to tell me that my daughter's mother was arrested for buying heroin with the kids in the car. I felt somewhat guilty, she lost the kids, and temporary custody was awarded to my mother. I was able to see my daughter for a little while, but I couldn't feel any emotions. Anything that felt abnormal I would just drink and drug to numb myself. It got to the point that absolutely nothing could mask the pain, or take away the guilt and shame. Little did I know God was making a move on my life, and there was nowhere else to run with the devil. I had become defeated and it was time to surrender. I eventually turned myself into the Montgomery County Jail. It was one of the hardest things that I ever had to do. I was sentenced to two years in prison. I would've never imagined that God would grab ahold of me the way he did. So many things happened during the course of my incarceration. I was disowned by my family. I had only one picture of my daughter. I received no mail, only from my best friend in Virginia. I had finally reached rock bottom. I prayed one night, it was the most honest and unselfish prayer that came from my heart. I said, "Jesus! I have failed you miserably, and I can no longer do this on my own, I am giving you my all, please show me how to live." The most beautiful thing happened, and it happened in prison. These are accounts of my life, spiritual revelations, dreams and visions inspired by God. I stopped running with the devil, and began to walk with Jesus.

Lost Highway

At the age of eighteen, I owned a 1980 black Monte Carlo. My parents helped me buy this car to commute back and forth to work. At the time I had a good job doing heating and air. Although I spent a lot of time and money indulging in drugs and alcohol. I would drive this vehicle all over Dayton, I really thought I was something special the truth was I was destroying myself and was hell bound. One evening I was at some friend's house, having some beers and smoking some weed. My so-called friend asked me if I would give him a lift over to a female's house that was clear across town. Being that I was intoxicated, I agreed to do so. I drove him over twenty minutes away and dropped him off. I had beers in the front seat of my car so I continued to drink on my way back to Dayton. I went back to my so-called friend's house, continued to drink, and then about an hour or so later he called. He wanted me to come back and pick him up, so I got into my vehicle wasted at this point and made my way back to get him.

For my friends who are reading this, please understand that whenever you are drinking and drugging, believing what you think is a good time, mark my words, you are giving the devil full reign over your life. You are not in control, you have become the entertainment for demons. As I was driving back to pick my so-called friend up, I realized I had forgotten how to get back to where I dropped him off. I thought I was in the same neighborhood while looking at various houses trying to remember which one it was. While driving along a dark road I took my eyes off of the road and what was in front of me. I veered into a truck, and smashed the side of it. I cursed like it was the trucks fault for being where it was, and then just kept driving. I continued down the street of the neighborhood, took the last swig from a bottle of beer, then chucked it out the window. I pulled onto a main road, then drove toward a gas station I saw up ahead. At that time there were no cell phones, people used pagers also known as beepers. I was going to page my so-called friend to get directions back to the house he was at. I sat there inside of my car, thinking, "Wow, I just hit a truck!"

I just laughed it off. I looked out the driver side window from behind the steering wheel I noticed a truck pulling into the gas station. It stopped about fifteen feet away from me, the bed was filled with people as well as the cab. Being so drunk, little did I know it was the truck that I hit on the dark road. And because I didn't know it was this truck, I didn't know that these men were at the gas station to deal with me. I rolled down my window, I reached over into my center console and fumbled to grab a cigarette. I couldn't find my lighter, and as the men were approaching my car I asked one of them as he drew near, if he had a light. He replied, "Yeah, I've got a light buddy!" He pulled out a blunt instrument and struck me in the head with it. I remember seeing stars, I was then grabbed by the hair as the men pummeled my face and beat me with whatever weapon they had. I tried to scurry to the other side of my vehicle, but it just wasn't possible. It felt like a thousand fists were pounding me all at once. I don't know how long this beating took place, but I do remember hearing a voice of a female who screamed, "Stop it! You're going to kill him!"

In that very same moment I saw a huge flash of white light. I don't remember anything else after this happened, until I found myself on the highway gazing into my rearview mirror. In the rearview were flashing lights of a police cruiser. I pulled off the side of the highway, and turned off the radio. It was quite peculiar that the song playing was "Highway to Hell" by AC/DC. I had no recollection of where I was at, or what had happened to me. I looked into the rearview mirror once again only to see myself beaten bloody and in pretty bad shape. The officer got out of his vehicle and approached my window, when he got to the car he was shining the flashlight all over it. Apparently my car had taken a serious beating as well. After shining his flashlight in my face, he asked what happened to me.

I started to remember that I was beaten up, and said, "Some dudes are trying to kill me." He looked at me very concerned, actually it looked like it hurt his feelings to see me in such a bad way. The officer then told me the reason he pulled me over was because I flew past him and he noticed my wheel smoking. Apparently from where I had hit the truck I destroyed the driver side quarter panel and it was rubbing against my tire. The officer asked me if I knew where I was, I replied, "No."

He said that I was near Englewood on I-70. I had drove about twenty miles from that gas station, and hadn't remembered any of it. The officer was concerned about my wounds and injuries, so he called for a medic. He also tried to make a report, but I couldn't recall anything to give him any information. The paramedics arrived and patched me up. They also ran some tests to see if I had a concussion. According to them, I did not. After the medics had left the scene, the officer asked if I had any money. I had about twenty dollars, so he called a cab for me and arranged for my Monte Carlo to be towed. He could have easily charged me with DUI but he did not. When the cab arrived, I got into it and I remember him saying, "Son, I will pray for you." Could this officer have been an angel? Was it his mission to spare my life on this lost highway to hell? Often I still wonder about that huge flash of light, and the woman screaming, "Stop it! You're going to kill him!" Who was really driving my car? I don't think it was me. Only by the grace of God that officer would save my life on that lost highway.

Bipolar Roller Coaster

After being assaulted at the gas station, and blacking out, things just weren't the same for me. I had trouble retrieving memories, I would also have horrible headaches that sometimes lasted for days. Going to see a Doctor was something that rarely occurred during my childhood, and I would follow the pattern of neglect toward myself, into my adult years especially with all the dysfunction I was exposed to growing up. My mother said that my biological father had suffered from an untreated mental illness, but there wasn't any evidence to support that. I was told that mental illness can be passed down through generations. I was naïve to this, until after the accident and at the age of eighteen years old I was hospitalized for mania. My mind would race at 1,000 mph. I couldn't sleep nor could I eat. I had stayed up or nearly four days straight. I started becoming delusional, as if I was living in a movie and I could control situations and outcomes. I felt as if I were super human, except I didn't wear a cape or a funny suit. I was at odds with my stepfather, so I went to stay with my mother's sister for a couple of days. On one night, I was speaking to her and my good childhood friend. I was told that I was speaking in riddles and code that didn't make any sense. My aunt called my mother and said that I needed to get some help.

I was taken to the Miami Valley Hospital and willingly admitted myself, to the psychiatric unit. I had completely lost touch with reality. The nurses began taking blood and urine samples. At this point in my life I had nothing in my system. I spoke with the ER psychiatrist and whatever was said during our conversation, he then had me admitted to the psychiatric unit. During my time on the unit I would speak with counselors, psychologists and psychiatrists. I was given a cocktail of medications that kept me severely sedated. I stayed in the psych unit for a period of ten days. One psychiatrist would diagnose me as bipolar manic depressive. I was given prescriptions and a discharge summary for aftercare. I went to a few groups and took the medications until they ran out. Not having insurance nor having an understanding of how severe my addiction really was caused me to ride this bipolar roller coaster for over thirteen years. It seemed easier to mask my illness by self-medicating with booze and drugs, but when I ran out of that or money, my mind would become a very hostile place. I would then experience intense lows of depression.

I lost interest in things that would allow me to feel satisfied, and would sleep anywhere from twelve to sixteen hours a day. I always thought that I was different with my perception of life and reality. I never really talked to too many people about my mental illness. I wanted to go through life pretending that it didn't exist, or that the Doctors had no clue of what they were talking about. I think the drugs played a huge part in the disruption of my mental stability. It was usually after a weeklong binge of drinking and drugging I would either become manic or severely depressed. I remember one time being in an outpatient program I was speaking with a psychologist.

She said that because I had used cocaine for so many years, it would take several years for my brain to produce the natural ability of being happy. She was right, I would only feel a false sense of happiness under the influence of drugs or alcohol.

I experienced over a dozen hospitalizations as a result of my mental illness. I was also affiliated with over a dozen outpatient organizations. Every single time I would take the medication until it ran out, then self-medicate by getting loaded. While driving from Ohio to Georgia, I would experience one of the worst mental breakdowns I ever had. I was driving my 1997 Honda Prelude, I was very rough on the clutch to the point that it went out somewhere on a Georgia Highway. I pulled the car off to the side of the highway, in being angry I pushed the gas pedal to the floor.

I held it there until the engine blew up. I then went and sat on the hood of my car, and waited for about twenty minutes until a police officer came. I don't remember exactly what happened, but I do remember the officer having my car towed and I was taken to some hospital in Georgia. As I sat on a gurney within the ER, I began to think the hospital staff were plotting some evil agenda against me. I had become completely paranoid, impatient, and angered to the point I started leaving the hospital. The nurses tried to stop me and then called security. I left the hospital and walked up to a busy road. I had no idea where I was, or where I was going.

Traffic was heavily congested, I walked down the road as though I was invincible. I guess it caused one motor vehiclist to become concerned and call the police. After walking about a half mile, I arrived at a department store. I went to the pay phone and tried to call my best friend. As soon as I got on the phone, a police officer would pull into the parking lot, and then escort me back to the hospital. From the hospital I was then transferred to a state psychiatric facility in Augusta, Georgia. It reminded me of something similar to a scene out of *One Flew over the Cuckoo's Nest*. I thought the staff were part of some voodoo occult, that were conspiring against me to place a voodoo hex causing me to suffer. One night I became aggressive toward the staff, to the point I was wrestled to the floor and given a shot to knock me out. I don't know how I ever made it out of that hospital? After spending nearly two weeks there, I was released once again with a cocktail of psych meds, prescriptions, and instructions for aftercare.

Somehow or another I began to get somewhat of a handle on how to keep my psychosis at bay. Of course I wasn't taking the medications I was prescribed, I just figured out a new way of using street drugs to combat the symptoms. I couldn't prevent the intense lows of depression or the feelings of worthlessness that lead into suicidal thoughts. The easiest way to escape these feelings was sleep, I would have slept my entire life away if my mind and body would have allowed it. It wasn't until I went to prison that I began to take a serious look at my mental illness.

Being sober and of clear mind, has shown me the evidence to support I had a chemical imbalance within my brain. Was this caused by drugs? Or was it the bad hand I was dealt with genetics? I really didn't know, and I'm not sure if the doctors really knew? I just knew that I had better start living in the solution. I began taking medications while in prison, until I turned my life over to Christ. I knew that God was fully capable of performing a miracle, and healing me of my struggles. So I stopped taking the medications. I couldn't see just how unstable I would come across to other people, in my mind I felt okay.

It wasn't until I went to the hole and was mandated to take my medications that I saw the significant importance of taking them. I began working closely with the prison psychiatrist. I became completely vulnerable to them, disclosing the innermost details of how I thought, felt and acted during mania or in a state of depression. I was diagnosed bipolar with a schizo affective disorder.

I truly believe that many doctors can over prescribe medications for many possible reasons:

1. They really don't know what they're doing.
2. They receive financial kickbacks, from pharmaceutical reps.
3. It's easier to prescribe a cocktail of medications and wean out what isn't beneficial.
4. Their caseloads are so overwhelming, that they don't have the available time to fully establish a relationship with their patients.

I also truly believe that Christ is the ultimate physician and healer, but I also believe that Christ gave us doctors to assist us in those healing processes.

It reminds me of an old fictional tale I had heard several times:

Once there was a man who was shipwrecked within the ocean. A boat came by and saw him floating within the water, they offered him a life raft and to come aboard. He said, "I'll be fine, Jesus will rescue me!" So the boat left and he continued to try and stay afloat.

Next a helicopter would fly overhead, and hoist down a ladder. The man once again would say, "I'll be fine, Jesus will rescue me!" So the helicopter flew away, and he continued to try and stay afloat. Eventually he would drown, and then was ascended into heaven before the throne of Jesus.

As the man stood before Jesus, he asked him, "Lord, why did you let me drown?"

Jesus replied, "My son, who do you think sent the boat and the helicopter?"

This simple fictional tale would help me stay focused on managing the symptoms of my illness. I still take my medication as prescribed and meet with a therapist once a month. I also meet with a psychiatrist once every three months. By my doing this I haven't experienced any major mental meltdowns. Taking medication is not the cure-all in coping with life, on its own terms. I still struggle with anxiety; but by working out it not only helps with the tension, it also diffuses my anger. I still have short bouts of depression; the difference today is that I force myself to be productive. Even a small amount of effort can go a long way. Never be ashamed to admit you struggle with a mental illness, it wasn't your choice. Working with the right doctor and consistently taking the right medication without the use of drugs or alcohol can allow you to live a beneficial life, and calm the storms within.

The Snake, the Watch, and the Cross

It was April 12, 2002. The very next day I would be turning twenty-three years old. At that time, I was in a band called Chalkboard Symphony. I stayed in a house with a guy who used to come to all our shows. A lot of parties occurred in this house, and what seemed like an awesome time, was actually the deceit of the devil. I had birthday plans for the very next day, so in my mind I wasn't going to do anything to sabotage them. I was just sitting at home watching TV and at about 9:30 p.m., there was a knock at the front door. I answered the door, and it was my little sister with one of her girlfriends. They were standing outside the door holding bottles of liquor, my little sister smiled real big and said, "Happy birthday, Bubby!"

She came inside gave me a big hug, we sat down at the kitchen table as her friend began pouring drinks. I was very happy to see my little sister, it was a pleasant surprise. I didn't approve of the other girl she had brought with her, but welcomed her anyways. My sister then began saying, she and her friend had a surprise for me. The other girl pulled out a large bag of what appeared to be cocaine. Considering I lived in the grips of my addiction to cocaine, I just couldn't say no, even though I had plans the next day. That white powder, also known as Devil's Dandruff, ruled my decision-making. At this time in my life, Jesus was the furthest thing from my heart. I believed in him, but I wasn't ready to live for him by any means. My sister, her girlfriend, and I sat at the kitchen table, drinking and snorting drugs until the wee hours of the morning. My sister said at one point during the night, that my stepfather wanted to see me on my birthday and that he had baked a cake and bought a gift for me.

I really didn't care to go to my stepfather's, however I told my sister I would.

As the sun began to rise on April 13, 2012, I said to my sister you had better get going. I also said that if your father finds out you were over here doing drugs with me, it would be all bad. She and her friend left, she said to me once again, "Happy Birthday Bubby," and that she would be waiting on me to get to my stepfather's house. I had been up all night, and was feeling very abnormal from all the cocaine and alcohol. I jumped in the shower, tried to relax for a little while, and then called my stepfather. I told him I would be headed to his house in the next couple of hours.

As I made my way there, I felt this presence of evil all around me. I wanted to turn around, but I did not. I got to the house and knocked on the front door, my stepfather greeted me, so I stepped inside. I looked around the house for my little sister, but didn't see her. I sat down on the couch, then looked over to see my stepfather's new girlfriend. She was actually a former friend of my mother's. Whenever my mother was beaten by my stepfather, this was the same woman that we would flee to.

What a friend she was, to shack up with my abusive stepfather after my mother divorced him. But that's for God to judge, not me. While the girlfriend sat on the love seat across from me, I noticed that she was fondling a small garden snake. Something didn't settle right in my spirit, it was as though she was mesmerized by this little evil creature. My stepfather then came over and sat on the couch next to me, I asked him where my sister was, and he said she was asleep in bed. I couldn't help but think to myself, I wonder if he knows where she was at last night? I wonder if he knows that I spent all night partying. The mood of the house was very uncomfortable, I couldn't quite understand why I was feeling the way I did. Something in my spirit was telling me, something very wrong is going on in here. I had done drugs enough to know when I was just being paranoid, and this situation was something totally different. My stepfather and his girlfriend started going through the motions of lighting candles on a birthday cake. They asked me if I would like a piece, and I said maybe later, I'm not hungry right now. I looked over at the girlfriend, who once again was playing with the snake, she asked me, "Johnny do you like snakes?"

I said very sternly, "I hate snakes!"

She said to me, "Oh, what a shame I got this snake for you." She then said that she was working in her garden, when she discovered the snake and was going to kill it. I thought to myself, Wow! That's really nice you were about to kill a snake and thought of me. She then said while laughing, "I was going to behead it, but thought you might've liked it." In that moment I wanted to lash out and tell her just how demented I thought she really was. Out of respect I only said, "Well it looks like you have yourself a snake." She appeared to be discouraged that I didn't take it. She put the snake away, and said that she had another gift for me. After the woman tried to give me a snake, I really didn't want anything else she had to offer.

She handed over a little wrapped box to my stepfather, he then gave it to me and I unwrapped it. Inside of a clear jewel case was a small cross. It was the most unpleasant looking cross, I had ever seen. It was metal, and the edges were very jagged, it looked as though it would cut you. On it were five engraved Xs. My spirit was telling me, something was very wrong with this cross. I never took it out of the case, I only looked at it. I did notice that the cross inside of the box looked very greasy. I looked up to see my stepfather's girlfriend, she gave me a smile that was almost wicked. She proceeded to tell me that the cross was blessed with the prayer oil of Padre Pio. I had no idea who that was, but I later found out that he had suffered from stigmata. Stigmata was a supernatural occurrence that resembled the crucifixion of Jesus.

Padre Pio suffered from holes in his hands that never stopped bleeding. Here I sat and thought to myself, "Who is this woman to bless anything. What's really going on here?" I continued to sit on the couch, even though I was ready to go as soon as I stepped through the front door. I put the jewel case on the coffee table, as I was doing so my stepfather said, that he had a gift for me. Because I was in a rock 'n' roll band at that time I wore my hair fairly long and it was dyed jet black. My stepfather started making jokes about the way I looked, then handed me a small box. I unwrapped it, and then opened it. It was a watch that had an all-black face, on a nickel chrome wristband. Sarcastically he said, "John the watch matches your hair!" while laughing. I can't stand sarcasm, it is an indirect way either to hurt someone's feelings or insult them. I became angry, after all this was my birthday. He looked over to his girlfriend who once again was seducing the small garden snake. They looked at each other, like this was a plot against me. Then my stepfather turned to me and said, "Johnny, I got you the watch to wear around your neck!" While laughing.

In that very moment my spirit grabbed ahold of me, but my flesh would react also. I became enraged, I got up then stormed out of the door slamming it shut behind me. I stepped away from the house, and I still had the watch in my hand. I turned around and threw it at the house, then made my way on foot up the street. I was so angry as I got about thirty to forty feet away my stepfather came out of the door saying, "Johnny Wait!"

I kept going and he said, "Johnny, please wait." So I turned around still very much angered, I could tell, that he was scared. I asked him, "So what's really going on here?" He tried to convince me that it was all an overreaction to my imagination. To this day, I still don't think that. His girlfriend was involved in some very ungodly practices. White magic or Black Magic, if it's not from the Word of God then it's all evil. There are things that just shouldn't be messed with. People open doors that allow demon forces to infiltrate their lives and the lives of others.

Doors they do not know how to shut. The Word of God speaks of what will happen to these types of people. My stepfather gathered the gifts and put them in a small gift bag. I didn't even want them but I took them thinking of how I had a friend even though he was Catholic, knew of someone studying to be a priest. I don't follow Catholicism. I am a Christian who believes in Genesis through Revelations.

However, the next day, I took the gifts to him and explained what transpired on my birthday. He looked at the cross and he also thought it appeared very demented. He said he had not seen anything like it before, he also stated that he had seen many different variations of the cross. He also believed that they were trying to place some kind of hex on me. I won't mention what it was, because it's irrelevant. He suggested that we pray against whatever evil that came along with those gifts. After we had prayed, we buried the cross and the watch. I really don't know what my stepfather and his girlfriend were up to that day, but I just don't believe it to be something of my wild imagination. It was evil, and I felt it. Friends, if you find yourself in the midst of people who practice witchcraft, sorcery and magic, flee from them! Then immediately pray that God gives you the ability to discern these types of people. Plead the blood of Jesus Christ with authority! Resist the devil, and he must flee from you.

The Basement

Growing up I had a very close friend named Robbie Pearce. Robbie lived with his dad, Dick, a.k.a Richard. Dick wasn't actually Robbie's dad, Robbie's mom had given him up to her parents, which were actually his grandparents. When he was very young the grandfather murdered the grandmother and then committed suicide. Dick was the brother of the murdered grandmother; that made Dick Robbie's great uncle. Robbie had a lot more freedom than all of us other kids, he also felt the need to please everyone. Dick managed a go-go bar, and would leave huge amounts of money throughout the house. Robbie would always find it, then treat his friends to pizza, arcades, movies or whatever. As a child I used to ride my bike up to Robbie's house. I would race up the street, fly into his yard, and then jump off of my bike onto his porch.

The bike would basically land wherever it wanted, I would then enter the house and head toward Robbie's room which was in the basement. We would watch MTV, play video games, and dream about the ideal girl we thought we would marry. We really didn't know anything about drugs during these years. We did some bad things, but at that time we were fairly good kids. I often would go to Robbie's house to hang out with him, I always came the same way usually on a bicycle. After years passed, Robbie and I grew apart. He started hanging out in a different circle, and became involved with using hallucinogens. I too started hanging out in a different circle and started using all kinds of drugs. I wouldn't see Robbie for quite a long time, I heard he took on a nickname and became a drug dealer. Everyone called him Keebler, like the cookie elves. I would hear about him from time to time, and that he met a girl that I went to high school with.

The two of them would have two sons. Sometime in 2002 or 2003 I was in the midst of some legal trouble. I had a warrant for my arrest, and was laying low at a buddy's house in East Dayton. On one evening, I sat on the front porch of the house. I noticed this woman walking toward me, she stopped at the front porch and had two awful black eyes. She appeared to have been beaten up pretty badly. After looking at her more closely, I noticed it was the girl I went to high school with that was dating Robbie. She asked me for some money, later I would find out she was smoking crack. I told her I didn't have any money, at that time I never had any money because I was a drug addict too.

I said to her, "Do you remember me?"

And she said, "Yeah!" I asked her where Robbie was and how was he doing? She informed me they were no longer together and he had full custody of their two boys. She said he lived just a few streets away from where I was hiding out. She suggested that I go see him, and that he had talked about me throughout the years. She then said she had to go, but I never bothered to ask her how she got the black eyes. I felt really bad for her, and I thought about Robbie. I thought about those boys and about their innocence. Robbie was a drug dealer in the ghetto, raising two kids on his own.

In fear of being arrested, I left for Virginia to where my best friend was living with her parents. Her father was a pastor and her mother worked for the church. I would attend Sunday services while I was there, my best friend's father would preach the word with such an anointing. They made me feel very welcome in their home, but I had the itch to find another band so I could continue to live wild and reckless. I searched the internet night after night, looking and listening to different bands. I found a band called Hereafter out of Winston-Salem North Carolina. I left immediately, and started staying in the home of the bassist. I'm not really sure of how many months had passed after seeing Robbie's ex-girlfriend? I hadn't even given much more thought about Robbie after leaving Ohio. One night after band practice, I fell asleep during a movie and this is what happened:

I was riding my bicycle up the street, very fast toward Robbie's house. The only difference was I was no longer a child, I was a grown man. I raced into the yard, jumped off of the bike, onto the front porch the same way I had always done. I approached the screen door and looked inside. In the living room sat Robbie's dad, Dick. He had a blank expression on his face, sitting on the couch, just staring at the wall. I called in through the screen door, saying, "Hey, Dick, it's Johnny. Where's Robbie?" He said nothing, but waved me in.

He just stared at the wall, then said, "He's in the basement getting ready to go."

I said, "Go where?"

Then he said, "He's been waiting for you in the basement."

I replied, "Okay then." I walked through the living room, through the kitchen, toward the door of the basement. As I stood in the doorway I looked across the house and saw that Dick had put his hands to his face, was hunched over and started crying. I went down into the basement, it was like it always had been. It smelled of dank mildew and was poorly lit. From the stairs I passed through the laundry room, toward Robbie's room. I drew back the bed sheet that acted as a door, then stepped inside. I looked around the room, and at first I didn't see Robbie. Then he rose up from near his bed, while frantically folding clothes and putting things into boxes. I was cheerful to see him, I hadn't seen him in ages.

I said, "Hey, bro, what's going on? Where are you going?"

He said, "I'm just putting some things away, because I'm going away for a while.

I just kind of laughed and said, "Well, where are you going?"

Again he said, "I'm just going away for a while." He stayed busy folding clothes and stuffing things into boxes, what was in these boxes I really don't know? After feeling confused about why he couldn't tell me where he was going, I began to notice something strange. The walls of the basement began turning into dirt, then the whole basement began turning into dirt. Suddenly, a door appeared on one of the dirt walls. The door looked as if it had been scorched and withstood fire, it had the look of an old chamber door. I just stood near the bed sheet doorway, mesmerized. I looked at Robbie, and his countenance had suddenly changed to sadness. The door opened, and out of it came six very aggressive looking men. These men were in very good shape, and it appeared they were all about their business. What that business was, I guess I'll never know. They glanced at me, but acted as though I didn't exist.

They surrounded Robbie, and for the final time, Robbie would say, "I'm going away for a while."

After all the folding of clothes, and stuffing things into boxes, I figured Robbie would take these things with him. But Robbie didn't take anything with him. The men grabbed him by the arms, and walked him through the open chamber door. The door stayed open long enough for me to take a look inside. I saw a dark tunneled out hallway, made completely of dirt. I watched them walk through it, until I could no longer see them. The door then slammed shut on its own. As I stood in front of it, the door disappeared and the basement returned back to its normal state. Robbie was gone, and I just stood there puzzled. I went back through the basement, to the stairs, up the stairs, and eventually made my way back into the living room. Dick was wailing, at this time. I didn't even say a word to him, I just walked out the door, found my bike and rode away down the street.

The next morning I woke up and couldn't help but think about Robbie, as I drank my cup of coffee. I was really disturbed by my encounter in his basement. A little while after waking up, the telephone rang. It was my mom, calling from Dayton, Ohio.

She said, "Johnny, brace yourself." Any time my mom had said this to me, it typically was bad news. She continued to say, "Last night Robbie Pearce was murdered!" She started crying and said, "I remember him being just a little boy, just a little boy!" After my mother settled down, she informed me that Robbie started dating a girl whose father did not approve of him.

The father did not approve of his daughter dating a drug dealer. That previous night, Robbie went to pick the girl up at her father's house. Aggressive words were exchanged, so the girl's father grabbed a shotgun, and shot Robbie in the head as he was running away. Witnesses say that Robbie lay in the yard, awaiting paramedics for quite some time. Robbie died. There is no doubt in my mind, that Robbie was saying goodbye to me. Why God allowed me to see this opens the door to so many things, in regards to salvation. It was a warning, yet I still continued to engage in a lifestyle of chaos. Where Robbie was going I do not know, but it didn't look like a good place. There certainly wasn't any indication of that tunnel being a path to heaven.

I don't know if Robbie was saved. I never remember him going to church, or mentioning Jesus. I do know, that he died in the trespasses of sin. It breaks my heart to think about Robbie, and especially those two boys. I loved Robbie, he was my childhood friend. He suffered his entire life, I just pray he is not in the eternal suffering. For those of you reading this take heed, if the drugs don't kill you! The lifestyle will!

Rear-View Smiling

I often thought about the night my, little sister passed away. The rain was pouring down the hardest I had ever seen in my life. After I got the phone call that my mother, my sister and some other unknown person were involved in a tragic car accident. Being told, "Your sister died" still echoes through my soul. I immediately ran out of the house, into the rain, into the storm while yelling at the sky saying, "No!" I would later go visit the scene of the accident, I climbed up the embankment underneath the bridge, and created the vision in my mind. I would sit there and cry. I would torture myself with the same ritual, for quite some time. Whenever I was drunk, I would go to the bridge and sit under it wishing it would have been me instead of her. That night on July 31, 2004, my mother, my sister and some unknown young man had left a bar in my mother's Lexus SC300. The rain was falling so heavily, that my mother lost control of her vehicle.

The car hydroplaned, she ran over the curb, and hit a bridge pillar on the rear driver's side. Upon impact it shattered all the windows, then spun the car around, and up the embankment under the bridge. My sister was ejected out of the back window, she sustained traumatic injuries that led to her death. When I first went to the bridge I found bloody clothing, one sandal that she was wearing, and also a chain belt that was broken into pieces. My heart was broken, to discover that there were flyers all over the road and in the grass as far as I could see. My mother had missing person's photos of my sister that were in the trunk of her car. My parents were supposed to pass them out, when my sister had went missing before she was arrested for prostitution of crack cocaine. I felt so sad as I collected all that I could from the scene of the accident.

On those nights that I would sit under the bridge sometimes I would feel a little comfort. I would envision Angels being all around my little sister that night right before she died. There was a church about fifty yards from the bridge pillar my mother hit. I would envision God's angels waiting in his holy house, for their time to comfort my sister. I prayed she did not suffer. At times I would feel her spirit, it would hurt because there was so much that I never got to say. I don't really know if my mother was intoxicated that night. It really doesn't matter anymore, that is between God and my mother. All I know is that I love my mother very much and I know my sister loved our mother very much. Who was I to judge my mother, especially after all the countless times that I drank and drove? I often would think about my sister, and her smiling in the rearview mirror. I even had visits from her after she passed away.

One night she appeared like this:

I was at a childhood friend's house, a kid I used to hang around with when I was about twelve years old. I was standing in the front yard of his house, when suddenly my mother pulled up in the same vehicle she was driving in the accident. I was a grown man, but everything else in this dream had the look and feel of 1992. She stopped the car in front of the house, rolled down the window, and said, "C'mon, Johnny, get in." I got into the car and pulled down the sun visor that had a mirror built into it. As I looked into the mirror, I saw the reflection of my little sister as she sat in the back seat. She was smiling, but didn't say a word. I didn't even acknowledge her being dead, I turned around in my seat and said, "I love you, Nay Nay!" She just smiled. I turned back around to look at my mom, then looked into the center console where the cup holder was, inside of it was a beer. I instantly turned my gaze from the can of beer toward my mother. I scolded her, yelling, "What are you doing? Don't you know you could kill her?" I turned around again to see my sister, she was still smiling. My mom hit the gas, and sped down the street, she was driving very fast. I was yelling and demanded that she let me out of the car.

The street we were on was directly behind the street I grew up on. We had only traveled about a block then turned the corner. I yelled once again to let me out of the car! She stopped at the corner of our street, the sun visor was still down, I looked into it once more and said, "I love you sis." She was still smiling and never said a word. I got out of the car, started up a small hill toward my stepfather's house. I took a few steps then looked behind me to see my mother in her vehicle speeding down the street. My sister turned around from the back window, she looked at me and smiled until they disappeared.

Widow Maker

After joining the band Edge of Life in Middletown Ohio, I was introduced to many different people. I would engage in large amounts of drug use and although I had a girl-friend in Dayton, I had a huge problem with promiscuity I recognize now, what drove me to do the things that I did. For all those that I hurt, conned, and manipulated I sincerely apologize. I also sincerely apologize to the amazing woman who tried to stay with me, as I destroyed myself while trying to destroy her. They say that misery loves company. There was not a single material thing, drug, woman, or even music that could fill the emptiness inside of me. Neither could it remove my afflictions, or take me out of my bondage.

Throughout my life, I desperately yearned for a dad, someone I could look up to like a dad. One night while at a party, I went into the kitchen of the house. There were a lot of people socializing in different areas. Some of the people there knew who I was, being the vocalist for Edge of Life. I was introduced to a guy named Tracy by the hostess of the party. At that time in my life I had a pretty cocky attitude. He said hi to me and seemed pretty eager to conversate, I pretty much gave him the rock-star ego complex. I would see Tracy again at different shows and other parties. We never really talked too much at first.

On another night at a party, I walked over to this girl's house who lived just a few doors down. The party I was at was running out of dope and booze, so I was hoping there was some at her place. As I entered the girls house, there were a few people sitting around in the living room snorting cocaine. Tracy happened to be one of those people. I eagerly wanted to talk to him now, because of what he had.

I had to feed the demons. I was welcomed into the small circle with an alcoholic beverage and a line of cocaine.

Tracy looked at me and said, "Well if it isn't Mr. Rock Star!" By no means was I a rock star. The truth was, I was a bottom-feeder. Tracy and I began to have a conversation, and as the night went on we grew to really like each other. We talked until the wee hours of the morning, up until the last line of coke and the last drop of alcohol was gone. I then would feel like a vampire, running from the sun in search of my coffin. I exchanged phone numbers with Tracy; he was in the process of starting his own landscaping company. He said that if I ever needed to make any extra cash, to give him a call. I couldn't hold a job, and I didn't like to work, only enough to support my addiction.

One day I called Tracy, and he came over to the house I was staying in. It was my bassist's house that I had to myself, because he lived with his girlfriend. When Tracy entered the door he was reaching into his pocket and pulled out a bag of coke.

He asked if I had a beer, and I didn't because I never had anything. I got high with Tracy, but in reality I got low with Tracy. We left the house, got into his truck and headed to a job site. While on the road Tracy popped in a CD of a Christian rock band. He turned it up really loud started to sing along. He asked me if I listened to any Christian music. I said I've listened to some, from time to time. Bands such as POD, Collective Soul, and Creed. But I considered these bands to be mainstream, not necessarily Christian. I began to think to myself, this dude is a complete hypocrite! Here we were snorting coke, listening to Christian music and headed to a job site. Little did I know God was at work, even in the midst of our trespasses. I felt a lot of guilt and shame by the words coming through the speakers. I asked him to turn the stereo off and put in another CD?

He said, "What's the matter, bro? Don't you love God?"

I loved God. I just couldn't handle the conviction of the Holy Spirit. Finally we arrived to the job, we completed the work and at the end of the day Tracy would say, "What do I owe you?" We would figure out the wages, then deduct the amount of drugs I used.

Needless to say, I didn't leave with much cash. I continued to spend a lot of time with Tracy. He was quite a bit older than me, and I guess I kind of looked at him like a father figure. We would go fishing, go to concerts, and hang out with his sons. He was a father of three boys, one in his teens, another was nine or ten and the baby around two years old. Tracy lived with his mother, she was a very sweet elderly Christian woman. After long days of work and long nights of drinking and drugging we would then go to his mother's house she always had food prepared and if it were a Saturday night she would sweetly say to Tracy, "Are you going to be ready for church tomorrow?"

Then he would say to me, "Johnny, you're welcome to go too!"

I would just smile, laugh it off and say, "Thanks." Tracy and I would then head up to his room, and I would fall asleep on the floor.

After about two hours of sleep Tracy would wake me up and say, "What are you going to do, man? I've got to get ready for church."

I would say, "Take me home. I'll go some other Sunday." This became a regular thing. Tracy always went to church and talked about Jesus. No matter how much wrong he was doing, Tracy without a doubt knew the love of Jesus.

Tracy would continue to invite me to church, I would always say no but deep down I didn't feel worthy of going. I still thought Tracy was a hypocrite. Tracy would always smile and say "He's waiting on ya, bro!" My bandmates didn't like all the time I would spend with Tracy. The cocaine started taking its toll on my voice, and I wasn't performing up to their standards. My bassist in Edge of Life would say, "Johnny, you're spending too much time with Tracy. He's been getting high for a long time, and, man, Tracy is no spring chicken. Johnny, mark my words, he is going to die." It made me angry, how dare they persecute Tracy after all the drinking and partying they did. I didn't think they were concerned with Tracy, they just wanted to preserve my voice in hopes of landing a record deal. But I continued to hang out with Tracy. One afternoon we were mulching some flowerbeds of a man that had loaned Tracy the money to start his business. Tracy said he couldn't pay me but he would supply the drugs if I stayed working. It was summer and scorching at 90°. We were killing ourselves out there, that and the devil was trying to kill us.

We were nearly to the point of heat exhaustion, then we finally took a break. Tracy became pale white and his nose began to bleed. He then blew his nose and out of it came the largest bloody pinkish flesh. Tracy would say, "Man does that burn!" I thought to myself, dear God this man needs some serious help. I then said to Tracy, "Man, I think you need to go to the hospital!"

He replied, "No, I just need to call it a day."

I loaded up the truck, and we drove off.

Tracy took me home and said, "I'll see you tomorrow."

He drove away, and I prayed that he wouldn't die. Tracy didn't die that night, we continued to get high, plant flowers, spread mulch and talk about Jesus.

One day I said to Tracy, "Dude, you know I love ya, if I followed Jesus the way you talk about him and we could stop getting high, we could change the world!"

I told him, "We're dying, Tracy!" God was speaking through me that day, and I just didn't recognize his voice even though he was using my own. He was trying to save us! After the death of my little sister I started spending more time in Dayton, Ohio. I would call Tracy from time to time. It wasn't long after struggling to stay clean, that I relapsed and started hanging out with a group of people in Dayton.

I met a couple girls, one of them I briefly dated and the other one I introduced to Tracy. Tracy was a very heartbroken man, who constantly yearned for his ex-wife. She left him for another man, shortly after having his youngest son. I felt his pain of losing his wife, very much like I would do Tracy would attach himself to just about any woman to feel wanted. That feeling was always a mirage, you would go to the ends of the earth to reach it, but it was never there.

Tracy and the girl whom I introduced him to started spending a lot of time together. Around this time, I was spending a lot of time alone grieving the death of my sister. One afternoon on my cell phone Tracy called me, he sounded really happy. He also sounded really concerned, because he found out that I started smoking crack. I don't really remember our conversation but I do remember him saying, "Johnny, he's waiting for you." Referring to Jesus. We said our goodbyes, and then I hung up the phone.

A couple of weeks later I was with that group of people in Dayton snorting coke. My cell phone rang, sometime in the early morning. It was some girl and she said to me, "Johnny, I have been trying to find your number and where you've been?"

"Johnny, I have horrible news!"

I said, "Who is this?" She said her name, and it was the girl I introduced Tracy to.

She then said, "Tracy died today."

My heart sank. I took all the cocaine that was sitting before me, and threw it across the room. I couldn't even cry because I was so high and numb. I found out later, Tracy had died on the field at one of his softball games. He told his coach that he wasn't feeling well, and was going to take a break in his truck. He stepped off the field, and then collapsed. He died of a heart attack called "the widow maker."

When it was time for the funeral, the night before I stayed up all night. I was drinking, smoking crack in mourning the death of my friend. I arrived at the funeral drunk, and out of my mind. I watched and stared at his family as they grieved. It was in September that Tracy died and I distinctly remember the song "When September Ends" by the band Green Day playing during the funeral procession.

Tracy's ex-wife arrived with their two-year-old son. His other two sons went to their brother and her, then walked to the coffin. The older boys just stood there and looked at their lifeless dad, the baby just wanted to play with him. I watched as they put Tracy in the ground, next to his father that died. I left, and then went to drink myself into oblivion.

I would still hear Tracy from time to time saying, "Johnny, he's waiting on ya!" I pray to see my friend in the light of truth. And when I see him again, he will be glad to know that I finally, made it to church.

The Carnal Carnival

I was twenty-seven years old, my life had downward spiraled into the darkest place I never thought I'd make it out of alive. I was staying with my best friend, I was beaten spiritually, mentally, and physically by my drug use. There were many nights that I cried myself to sleep, I remember one night after doing so screaming, "Please, Father, Do not forsake me!" Shortly thereafter, a peace came over me and I was able to get some rest. I was coming off of a drug binge, and hadn't slept in days. But on this night, I feared I would never wake up, I fell asleep and this is what happened:

I was walking down a winding cobblestone road.

As I traveled along the path I looked unto the horizon to see a blood red sky, filled with smoke. Also there was a huge Ferris wheel suspended in the sky, spinning slowly. I felt a sense of fear, but at the same time I was motivated by my curiosity. I focused on the path that lay before me. I saw a strange little man, wearing a top hat, standing in front of a huge black curtain. He was standing in between two coffins, as I began to approach him he said, "Welcome, we've been expecting you."

He then said, "So which one will it be?" as he pointed to the two coffins.

Being that I am left-handed, I usually favor choices to my left. So I chose the coffin on the right. The strange little man opened the lid, as I went to look inside of it I expected to see myself. I thought to myself, "Oh dear Jesus, this is it!" But to my surprise, when I looked inside of it, there was a stairwell that descended into a hallway. I climbed inside of the coffin, and started down the stairs. As I got to the bottom of the stairs, I looked up to see the little strange man, and

51

he said, "Well go on, take a look around." Then slammed the lid of the coffin shut. I stood in the hallway, it was titled in a white ceramic that was almost reminiscent of a hospital hallway. There were only two ways to go inside of the hallway. Either a short right, or down a long corridor to the left. Once again I went to the right. I stood inside of a doorway that opened up into a huge room. Inside of the room were every imaginable treasured earthly possession. Classic cars, baseball memorabilia, Campbell's soup collectibles, vintage Coca Cola machines. Let me just say there was a lot of stuff in this room.

Nothing within the room applied to my interests, but I began thinking, "Wow, this is the kind of stuff people worship." Although I thought it was rather intriguing, I still knew it was meaningless stuff. I was still standing in the hallway, so I decided to journey through it. As I passed the stairwell, and continued along, I noticed that the tiles on the floor and walls were breaking, eroding and becoming discolored.

A short ways down the hall to my left, there was an opening. I looked in to discover people frantically running around in what appeared to be a laboratory. I couldn't see their faces, and honestly I don't even know if they were people. I do know that they were carrying beakers, vials, and they were running frantically in the midst of this darkened laboratory. In the middle of the laboratory stood a very tall man, wearing a lab coat. He wore glasses that rested upon the edge of his nose, while holding a clipboard. He appeared to be the overseer, he then looked up from his clipboard, looked at me over his glasses and said to me in a very deep and uncomfortable voice, "You know why you're here, don't you?" His question caused me to go into "warrior mode." The truth was, I didn't know why I was there, but my spirit told me I needed to be prepared. So I replied assertively, "Yeah, I know why I'm here!"

He then said, "Well then, continue to have a look around."

I did just that, I went further down the hallway and suddenly all the tiles had disappeared completely. The floor was dirt and the walls became dirt as well. I continued to walk through and thought to myself, "Dear God, what is going on here?" I started to notice holes in the walls tunneled out, about three to four feet in diameter.

I couldn't see inside of them they were only filled with darkness. As I came into the end of the hallway that had now turned into a tunnel, it opened up into a huge dome of dirt. Everywhere I looked there were the tunneled out holes. I started to think, these are wormholes but also a human body could fit inside of them? I became consumed with fear, because in that moment I felt completely alone. I didn't even consider to turn back around, and go to the stairwell. Neither did I run, I cautiously entered into the dome, scared but strong.

All of a sudden a haze of black began to fill the space of the dome. I've always had a fighter type of spirit, I started to feel the presence of something coming. Although there were no corners, I went to the furthest space I could find and pressed my back against the wall. As soon as I did, I started to hear groaning and unheard animalistic sounds, coming from the holes. Within a matter of seconds appeared these creatures from out of the holes. They were everywhere, they were in human form however they were nothing human. I have seen many horror movies throughout the course of my life before becoming the Christian I now strive to be.

These were demons, unlike anything I had ever seen. They moved and distorted their bodies ever so painfully. As they drew closer to me, they appeared to be a dark gray color, wearing soulless eyes. Their eyes were solid black and glossy, from them was almost a radiating glow. It radiated darkness, if only you could imagine that. They were the wailing and gnashing of teeth that the Bible speaks about. These demons wanted the flesh, their teeth were so horrific looking that I can't even begin to describe them. As I remained embraced against the wall, they began to close in on me. I was reminded by the thought of Jesus on Golgotha. I stepped away from the wall and placed my feet together, I then threw out my arms as if I were on the cross like Jesus.

With authority, I spoke to the demonic creatures and said, "I am saved, and you cannot have me!" In that very same moment as they were just inches away from me I felt a huge surge of power. I turned into light, and shot out of the dome in such indescribable power. It still blows me away today to think about, because I really felt all this. God was trying to tell me something. I believed that place to be an entry point into hell. It was a warning, would I take heed to it, or would I continue in my ways of suffering, only to enter into the eternal suffering? Or would I exercise the power of the Holy Spirit to save me from the sting of death.

Upon the Rock

Around the age of twenty-seven, I became very intrigued to know more about God and Jesus. Let me clarify that there is no separation between the Father, The Son and The Holy Spirit. You would have to read the Bible for yourself, to understand everything that was predicted of Jesus birth and his earthly ministry. My only guilt at this time was although I hungered to draw closer to Jesus, and all the evidence that had occurred in my life, supported he was so very real I just couldn't let go of my wicked ways. Drugs, sex, lies, and violence.

The age of twenty-seven was a spiritual tsunami for me. I received a message online from my former bandmates near Atlanta, Georgia. They wanted me to join their new project, I had nothing to hold onto in Ohio so why not? Everything in Dayton felt so painful, it wasn't Dayton itself; it was what dwelled inside of me. My best friend encouraged me to go, I felt as though God was encouraging me to go too, but the devil wanted me to stay in Dayton and suffer. Needless to say I left for Georgia, and joined up with the band. So much power came from the music we played, God began to channel lyrics from me that provided such a sense of healing.

We were going to name our album *Road to Recovery*, it would have proved to be an amazing record. One day my younger guitar player encouraged me to take a ride with him. He said to grab my notebook as he grabbed his acoustic guitar. We drove into a very remote location somewhere in Georgia that was absolutely breathtaking. I looked around in awe, and felt the presence of the Holy Spirit. I started thinking about my sister, and what she might be doing in heaven in that very moment. As we walked through the woods, I could smell the wildflowers and feel the peace of the lush green that surrounded me. Everything radiated with such beautiful colors, it made me think of how perfect God and his creation is. I thought about heaven and what it would be like. We arrived at a place in the woods that had a waterfall. We stepped onto a rock that looked very similar to a park bench.

My guitar player sat down and said, "What do you feel like doing?"

I sat my notebook on another rock that almost looked like a desk built to write on. I said to him, "Play something and really feel it!" He started into a riff that was absolutely beautiful! So beautiful it brought tears to my eyes. I still was thinking about my sister, and how I missed her so much.

As the last tear fell onto my notebook, I began to write:

Perfect World
For: Rene 11/23/83–7/31/04

Reflections in the rearview, I see you smiling. And when I feel all alone, it's you beside me. Memories paint a picture, of where I will find you. In such a better place, I know one day soon . . . Mend the broken bridge, and I'll cross over. Into the other side, where life's not over. I will see you there, all in due time. In such a better place, with peace in the light. One day soon . . . In a perfect world, we'll meet again. In a perfect world, our lives won't end. Free from all this fear, Wiping tears from our eyes! In a perfect world, there's no unsaid goodbyes . . . Break these chains we're holding with answers from this life. Start a brand-new story, leave the past behind. In this world decaying, open up my mind. Let me feel your laughter, to feel some peace inside! In a perfect world, we'll meet again. In a perfect world, our lives won't end. Free from all this fear, wiping tears from our eyes. In a perfect world, there's no unsaid goodbyes . . .

I truly believe that this song was handed from heaven. I continued to think about my life, my family, Jesus and the possibilities that lie in wait. I had stopped everything as far as drugs, sex, and violence were concerned. I really wanted to become a new creature in Christ. Fear was still plaguing my life. Due to how driven I was by my music, and different musicians throughout history I always told myself that I would die at the age of twenty-seven. Much like the musicians I looked up to Jimi Hendrix, Janis Joplin, Kurt Cobain, etc. Right before I was to turn twenty-eight, I started telling myself it was okay to have a glass of wine. The devil being such a worthy adversary, he once again would have his way with me. For people who may drink and have a hard time feeling a closeness to God. Let me assure you that alcohol is the biggest ploy in separating you from exercising the power of the Holy Spirit. Just look at our nation and statistics surrounding alcohol related accidents and crimes. Even though I had all the evidence I needed, I still continued drinking. One night after heavy drinking I went home and don't remember passing out. But I do remember this:

I was walking through a field that was full of flowers, flowers that I had never seen before. The grass was so green and bright that it looked as if it were glowing. I slowly walked through a pasture, and come up to a stairwell of various rocks. It was a long way up but I began to climb to the top. I stepped out onto a large rock that extended from a cliff. As I slowly approached the edge, I became full of fear. I looked out onto the horizon and saw that large dark clouds were rolling in. Lightning and thunder began to bang and crash, I remember it being so loud that it hurt my ears. The clouds were approaching at a tremendous speed, I continued to look out from the cliff and saw land on the other side.

Upon the land, I saw an army marching through the storm. This entire time I was scared to look down the cliff, but I did. All I could see was darkness and the storm was below as well. My fear put me into battle mode, all my senses were heightened. I could smell the rain, even smoke, the grass and the flowers. I felt something coming up behind me as I stood on the cliff. But I didn't turn around and take a look. As they drew closer, I crouched down to the very tip of the rock almost like an offensive lineman of a football team. I felt a hand touch my right shoulder. As soon as it did I felt perfect peace, my fear was instantly removed.

The most comforting voice spoke to me and said, "My son, are you ready?" I slightly turned my head to the right only to look at his hand. It had a large hole in the center of it, and the whitest garment I've ever seen, rested gently at his wrist. Why I didn't turn all the way around I do not know? I knew it was Jesus! I was ready to fight and die for him. But the battle was already won by the cross. As his left hand departed from my shoulder, I then dove from the cliff straight into the storm.

Voice of Sunshine

During my spiritual conquest while living in Georgia, many peculiar things took place. God had made himself very evident in my life. I would constantly seek out God's voice, to direct me where to go. This created a lot of conflict within me, because I had a hard time distinguishing what was my own voice in comparison to God's. At that point in my life I hadn't received the baptism of the Holy Spirit. Looking back on those years, I know now that the small inner voice I paid such close attention to, were also whispers of the devil. I spent a lot of time in a downtown area of the Georgian city I lived in. Drinking espressos, theorizing about God, and the Bible. I had a little 1987 Toyota Camry that I bought for $500. It was so badly rusted that it would've looked better just to have some seats, and a steering wheel attached to the frame. However this little car was a blessing, and it having over one hundred thousand miles on it I still drove it all over Georgia.

Sad to say it broke down; when it broke down, I too broke down. There was this country road that led into to the downtown area, I would walk this little road for miles, into another little city to pray and meditate. I started becoming obsessed with fasting and prayer. Altogether that was a good thing, however seeing things through spiritual eyes all the time equaled mania for me. I would walk this road day in and day out, up to a hill in this small Georgia city. I would pray, cry, yell and laugh. This was a place I could be myself.

The people that lived in the city were the most meek people I had ever met. I believed God was showing me where to make my future home. Having been on a two-week fast, while walking the road back and forth from the hill to the city, I had ran myself ragged.

I was grieving for my sister, I was grieving for the salvation of the world and feared it was coming to an end. I felt intense pain while thinking about what I had done to myself, and what we had done with God's creation. I would see a small child and cry, because I felt strongly that their innocence would be short-lived. I don't know why I was experiencing all these intense feelings, it was just something I prayed God would walk me through.

My journey from the road had led me back into the downtown area, I went and purchased a cup of coffee and sat outside of a church on a bench. It happened to be a Sunday in the midafternoon. I don't remember if it was a church service or a wedding I only remember the doors opening to the church and lots of fine dressed people coming out that seemed very happy. A group of beautiful young women started approaching the bench where I sat.

They weren't paying any attention to me, but I remember listening to them and they were saying what a great party they were going to go to. I overheard them saying there would be lots of alcohol, hot tubs, and all the hot guys would be there. These girls were absolutely beautiful, but in the same moment I overheard them, they were downright ugly to me. It hurt my heart to hear how they were speaking especially after just coming out of a church. I still wouldn't go to church, because of all the hypocrisy I thought took place in it. It's truly a shame that the devil can go in and out of the house of God as he pleases.

After hearing the young women talk I departed from there and walked around some more downtown. I had my Bible with me and eventually I went and sat under this huge tree and opened it up. Inside of it I kept the poem that my guitar player had given me. I hadn't read it up to this point but while sitting under the tree the world just seemed to race around me, I began to read the poem. It was about a little boy who was waiting on his father day in and in day out, but he never showed up. At the end of the poem, it spoke about how he never gave up on waiting for his father. An uncontrollable flood of tears started falling from my eyes, I looked up to see dad's pushing their kids, while in strollers into the park. Vehicles were driving by with what appeared to be fathers and sons laughing and having a good time. To me it was like, "Wow, God, what are you trying to tell me?" Could I be that little boy who still wasn't going to give up? Grieving for an earthly father, while yearning for my spiritual father. I was able to regroup my feelings, people looked at me as if I were bat crap crazy. Here was this grown man sitting under a tree with a Bible, crying his eyes out. I made my way through downtown and stopped at the corner of a street.

I noticed a small flyer that was attached to the side of a building. I read over it and I don't remember exactly what it said, I do remember it saying that it was inviting people to a local shop in the downtown area for a meet and greet. It just so happened to be on this very same day, and at the very same hour. As I stood there reading the flyer, two young women stopped at the corner while having a conversation waiting for the crosswalk signal to change. I don't know what they were talking about, but I remember looking at one of the women and as she looked at me almost in a childlike voice she said, "You should go check it out." Although she wasn't directly talking to me I tuned in to what she had said. The women crossed the street and as they were crossing I noticed the word "sunshine" written on the back of one of the women's shirt. I truly felt that God was using that young woman and leading me to the place listed on the flyer.

Once again I would look at the flyer, got the address and went. I was following the voice of sunshine. I approached a small storefront, walked inside and discovered it to be filled with religious artifacts, stones, and books. Basically it was the culmination of every imaginable doctrine and spiritual belief. I really didn't like these types of places especially with what had occurred on my birthday at my stepfather's house. I walked around the store very cautiously looking at things such as African voodoo artifacts, Buddhist shrines, and Native American jewelry. There was a small section in the store dedicated to Christianity, as I glanced over my shoulder I began to feel eyes all upon me. I felt very uncomfortable, I actually gave them an angry stare possibly even scaring the patrons of the store. A clerk then approached me and asked if I needed any help with anything?

I asked him what was the event being held mentioned on the flyer. He responded by saying that they were just wrapping up the first session and the second would be in about ten minutes. So I continued to look around the store staring at the crucifixes and the few things that pertained to Christianity.

The clerk then again came up to me and said, "It's about time, if you're ready?" I followed him through the store past a couple of rooms, I looked into one and saw a man lying on a table. There was a woman standing over him chanting words while placing stones all around his body.

Now what I'm about to say may be very controversial especially among Christian readers. First of all I need to assertively state that I am a Christian. I would not recommend venturing into these types of places. These types of places open doors into the spiritual realm that can be very dangerous. So please, be extremely cautious about what you expose yourself to. I continued past the room and was led to a small staircase.

The clerk then said, "She's in the upper room." My curiosity piqued me to see who she was and what was exactly going on? I went up the stairs, and stepped into the room. I looked around to discover there were three women sitting in chairs. In the far corner of the room was a large wooden statue of an Indian chief. Seeing the statue of the Indian chief brought me comfort. Due to the fact I had been on such a long period of fasting my discernment level was very intense. I studied the three women and one of them appeared not to like me. She seemed very uncomfortable by my being there. It was as though our spirits were battling without even saying anything. I remember her talking a hundred miles an hour about something I believe to be a Wiccan practice. I was angry to hear what she was saying, I think she knew that, she gave me a cold stare and eventually left the room. The woman that she was talking to appeared to be a Wiccan as well. Although I really wasn't sure about the woman who left the room, she appeared to be a student of the woman that had stayed.

The second Wiccan woman wore all dark clothing, she studied me very hard and when I would look at her very intensely in her eyes, she would look away. I've always kept a warrior type of attitude and even being a young believer, I was a soldier for Christ versus other religious practices. The woman sat in front of a large mirror that she kept gazing into. I thought to myself, what is so fascinating about that mirror? Or maybe she was just completely vain? Whatever it was, she would take glances at me through the mirror and never said a word.

The third woman was a very petite older woman. She wore glasses that gently rested on the edge of her nose. She radiated of peace, she was very gentle looking and I was instantly drawn to her. I said to her without even knowing the other woman in the room "How do you associate with people like that?" She looked at me, smiled and said, "Because I have to be peaceful with everyone." She then asked me to sit down. I told her that I was going to sit next to the Indian chief statue while laughing because he seemed safe. She looked at me and said, "Good choice." After I was seated the peaceful woman asked me my name, the Wiccan woman still had said nothing. I said my name is Johnny, and then she said, "Johnny, what brought you here today?"

Afraid of being honest I said, "I really don't know."

Her response was, "Well then, what can I do for you?"

Again I said, "I really don't know?"

She then said, "So, Johnny, then tell me about yourself?" I started with the basics, then became so comfortable everything had just started pouring out. I was dealing with so much emotional turmoil while being back and forth in my pursuit of faith that I needed someone to vent to. I really don't remember what I was saying, I truly don't even think I was the one that was talking. I kind of just went into autopilot. I do remember crying out and saying I just wanted to go home, but my home I was speaking of was heaven. I also said that I miss my little sister, and prayed that God would give me wings to fly far away from here. "It's all going to be over soon!" I said. I was crying my eyes out as the two women looked at each other.

The Wiccan woman still was not saying a word. She still continued to take glances into the mirror. I stopped crying and the peaceful meek woman asked me what I did. I told her I was a musician that moved from Ohio and was feeling all alone. She asked to hear a song, so with what little voice I had left after all the yelling and praying that I did on that small hill in that Georgian city; I began singing "Perfect World," the song I had written for my sister. I began crying again as I sang it my voice was ragged, my body physically exhausted. I had huge blisters and sores on my feet from all the nonstop walking up and down that country road.

After I was done singing the song the woman looked at me and stared for a moment, I felt a little relieved, but still could feel the hurt. The peaceful meek woman got up from her chair, came over to me and said, "Johnny, I have a gift for you."

I became really confused, even a little fearful but I chose to trust her. She told me to relax and take some deep breaths, she then said to close my eyes, and so I did. She then placed around my shoulders some type of fur item and gently brushed it along my neck and face. She said, "Feel the warmth, Johnny." "Johnny, feel the fire."

My eyes still closed, she then put her hands to my temples.

She said, "Okay, Johnny, you need to breathe and focus on the light."

And so I did; the room itself was already bright, but as she started massaging my temples, the light inside of my closed eyes began getting brighter, and I mean really bright. I was scared, I even told myself that I was dying and that this woman was an Angel who had come to take me home. I began to weep the light grew stronger and the woman again said, "Johnny, you have to breathe." The motions of her massaging my temples ceased, she said to keep my eyes closed and focus on my breathing. She began to talk to me and said, "Johnny, I now want you to slowly open your eyes."

And so I did. I felt peace, complete serenity; I just sat there thinking to myself who and what are you people? The Wiccan still hadn't said a word. The peaceful and meek woman asked how I felt. I said content, and she replied that God has blessed me with music and that my music would save people's lives. She told me that my life would never be the same, then with the most seriousness and boldness she said to me, "Remember, Johnny, you are not alone." She got up from her chair again, I couldn't help but start crying again, but this time, it wasn't from sadness. She came over to me and as I sat in the chair she hugged me with my head rested against her womb and bosom. She felt like a loving mother. She said I'm sorry the devil had control in your house, why she said that is beyond me? I really didn't share anything about my childhood but somehow she knew.

She held me a little while longer, then let go and said, "Remember, Johnny, your life will never again be the same." Now the Wiccan woman who hadn't said a word the entire time finally spoke and said, "I'm sorry for what's happened to you." She said I want to give you this while handing me a twenty-dollar bill.

She then said, "Johnny, please take care of yourself."

I was skeptical about taking the money, but I did. I smiled to the woman and said, "God bless you." I then left the room, down the stairs and through the store. It was nightfall so I journeyed to a Park bench to think about what had just transpired. I did not know what that gift was or if God had used that woman as a conduit to bless me with something great? Who was she really? I would never see or hear from her again. I did not know her faith, all I know is something very special happened in that upper room.

Many Christians especially the zealots may think negatively about this situation. I can't think of how in any way, shape, or form she contradicted the word of God. She never did mention Jesus, but whatever happened there, I believe I was protected by the Holy Spirit. I would have many experiences in that small Georgia town, some in which I cannot disclose because I don't think the world would understand. To this day I still don't understand it, but I'm sure that Jesus will one day reveal it.

Amazing Layla Grace

The morning of February 9, 2009, I would experience the greatest blessing I could ever receive in this world. I was an absolute nervous wreck while loading up the car, packing diaper bags, and folding little outfits for my little girl to wear home. Before going into the operating room I must've smoked nearly a whole pack of cigarettes within two hours. This really discouraged Layla's mother, I don't even think she really wanted me there due to my nervousness.

As I sat in the waiting room the nurses finally came to me and asked if I was ready? I said yes, with much excitement. I cleaned up, got dressed in scrubs, and was led into the operating room. As I began entering the operating room, I literally became enraptured into a state of eutopia. I really can't describe it, all I know is that it was like stepping into the unseen presence of angels and God. The doctors and nurses would ask me again if I was ready. Tears began to fall while music was softly being played over a stereo in the operating room. The song was a positively uplifting one by the band Goo Goo Dolls. I looked at Layla's mother prepared for surgery, I sat by her side and she asked, "Are you okay?" I couldn't even speak. The doctors said it was time and started the delivery, Layla Grace would be delivered by cesarean. I patiently and eagerly waited to see my little Layla. Layla's mom started to worry, she looked at me and said, "Johnny, something's wrong."

I said, "Don't worry she will be here any second." And not even seconds after I said those words, there she was! I know what I saw and felt, but as she presented herself into the world—literally the lights in the room became brighter. I felt this unexplainable presence all around me, I was there, but it felt as though I transcended into another dimension. Layla was more than an Angel in my eyes. She definitely was the physical representation of grace, something I did not deserve, but someone God chose to bless me with. I cut her little umbilical cord and watched as the nurses cleaned her up.

The protective father in me, thought they were being too rough as they took her weight and measurements. She was so delicate and fragile in my eyes. Layla would weigh, ten pounds and six ounces. The nurses joked and said, she could easily be the first female NFL player. After she was cleaned up and wrapped in swaddling clothes, they asked me if I was ready to hold her. I went and sat next to Layla's mom, and then they brought her to me and placed her in my arms. I just stared at her, and whispered while she slowly opened her eyes and looked into mine. A flood of tears began to fall, and the warmth of love began to fill my soul as we both curiously stared at each other. She was so pure, innocent and fresh from heaven. How could I have ever deserved such a precious gift? The day would arrive that we were able to take her home. I was so proud to bring her home, Layla's mother and I had her nursery prepared by painting it in a real pretty pink. Her name was on the wall just above her crib and the theme of her room would be teddy bears.

I was clean and sober; however, I was struggling to stay that way. I was also on some heavy psychotropics, which caused me to feel very awkward. I continued taking them as suggested by the doctor. During that winter of 2009, we were renting a house on a very busy road. I wasn't comfortable living there, especially with four children on such a busy street. Layla's brothers and sister were confined to only playing in the backyard, and I would freak out if I discovered they were in the front yard. God would bless our family once again. Being that it was winter, the children had to sleep downstairs because the upper rooms weren't properly heating.

I called the landlord, and to my surprise, he informed me that the house was in foreclosure. Apparently he was not paying the mortgage with our rent money. I was furious, scared, and concerned being that we had a newborn baby and would have to find somewhere to go immediately during the harsh winter. Layla's mom wanted to stay in the same school district, for the sake of the kids educations. I didn't care where we went, my only concern was having a stable home for my newborn daughter. By the grace of God, we found a little house on a dead-end road where cars traveling were not an issue. I didn't know at the time just how blessed we were, and how God knew exactly what we needed. Not only did he know what we needed, but he provided it. Like I said previously, I was struggling to stay clean and sober. I would regularly attend the meetings of Narcotics Anonymous, however I hadn't reached a full point of surrender.

I wasn't working and fulfilling my responsibilities to my family. I still had dreams, hopes, and aspirations, but it was hard for me to see myself being a family man. I knew that I loved my daughter very much, and how could I not? She was perfect in every way, she rarely cried and loved the sounds of music. I wonder where she got that from? My mother was a huge help in making sure Layla had everything she needed. I finally would find a job. It would be at a restaurant that was soon to open and many positions were available.

Just days prior to my interview, the devil and my own worst enemy of addiction would back me into a corner. In the rooms of NA, they say it is a corner that you won't come out of clean. I didn't acknowledge the presence of God working in my life at this time, I still thought I could do things my way. I wasn't able to feel anything in a spiritual sense except for Layla's birth. One afternoon Layla's mother and I started joking about purchasing some cocaine. This wasn't a joke at all, the truth was we were testing one another, because we both wanted to get high. We carried on teasing one another throughout the day, Layla's mom had been clean for a little over nine months, and it was just a little over six months for myself. That night it all went down the drain.

I had relapsed even before I purchased the drugs. The relapse happened in my thoughts, with the obsession. I manipulated the entire situation until my daughter's mother and I ended up snorting cocaine, all night long. Even in the midst of getting high, I felt intense guilt. My daughter lay asleep so innocently, while once again I would step right into the flames of hell with the devil. I hated myself for being so self-centered, self-seeking, and selfish. The sun began to rise, and the drugs had run out. My mentality was screaming for more! Layla's mother and I sat on the bed looking at each other, in shame. It wouldn't be long and the baby would wake up. The other kids were with their dad I looked at Layla's mom and said she had better get some rest. She moved away from me and while sitting at the edge of the bed she began to bawl her eyes out. She was crying and saying, "Johnny, you were clean for six months! And now we have this baby, what's going to happen now?" She continued to say how scared she was that Layla would not have a daddy.

It broke my heart to hear these things, but the disease of addiction had hit me full force, and I was right back to where I started. But this time, it would be worse. I would try to comfort her with lies, saying that I would contact my sponsor and get a white key tag at a NA meeting immediately. But the truth was, I was ready to continue getting high. I was choosing drugs over the precious, innocent, gift that I had received from God.

Of course I never made it back to a NA meeting. I eventually started working, Layla's mom would also get a job at the same restaurant as me. She would work day shifts, while I would work nights. We would get high almost every chance that we could, while the other kids would spend the weekend with their dad. It didn't take long for it to progress, and then we were getting drugs just about every day of the week. I hadn't started using heroin again, but I was using cocaine, Vicodin and Percocet's. Layla's mom would throw a fit, if I wanted to drink alcohol. She knew how violent I could become. As we continued to use, Layla would lose the unity of her mommy and daddy. The other children would witness the mental abuse and constant arguments from the mood altering chemicals we indulged in.

One afternoon I made a phone call to purchase some drugs, my acquaintance only had heroin, so without a second's thought I told him to bring it. I purchased it, and then waited for Layla's mom to get back from the grocery store. She came inside, and I said, "We need to talk, I did something you are going to flip out about." I then proceeded to manipulate her into using heroin with me. We already had a bad relationship, but on this day it was the beginning of the end. She was instantly hooked, at that time I felt no guilt, because it was all about me. It started to become very easy to put Layla in her swing, turn on the radio and just stare at her. She would just smile, she was a baby that could be content with just about anything or anyone. I wasn't giving her any of the attention, she deserved.

I would work long hours at the restaurant just to spend my money on heroin. My mother was always there to enable me in a pinch situation. I would lie about money that I would get from her that was supposed to be used for diapers and formula. I was a horrible father, I was failing her. I felt for Layla, but my actions spoke otherwise. Yet she was always overjoyed to see her poor excuse of a dad. My heroin use and my sinful lifestyle tore me away from my little girl, she was six months old when I received my first prison number. I got out right before her first birthday party, and I would attended it despite the restraining order her mother had placed on me. I started secretly using right away. It wasn't long before I was in jail, then in rehab, out of rehab, getting high again, violating the protection order, and then went on the run.

While on the run I tried to tell myself, I'm just going to erase her from my heart and mind, but it just wasn't possible. My guilt and shame kept me bound in my addiction. The fear of failing her, for her entire life seemed like the reality I would endure. Another man had stepped in to do the job that I was supposed to do. I had a cell phone that had some small video clips of Layla on it. I would watch them over and over on many sleepless nights. Crying, wishing I would just die or not feel anything at all. After finally being truthfully found out by the band in Nashville, I was forced to face my consequences. When I returned to Dayton I discovered that Layla's mother hadn't stopped using, and was busted for purchasing heroin with the children in the car. My mom was given temporary custody. I would try to hide out at my mom's; making my mother a nervous wreck. She had to be a parent again while harboring a fugitive.

The day arrived where my mother would pick up Layla and her things. I anxiously awaited for her to get back, and about an hour later the phone rang. It was my mother, and she was in the garage needing help to unload the baby and her things. I had butterflies in my stomach not knowing how Layla would react, would she recognize me? These quick intense scenarios were racing through my mind as I entered into the garage. I went to the passenger back seat, where Layla was. I looked at her and she looked back at me. I opened the car door as my mother said in a playful and happy voice, "Layla, there's your Daddy!"

Instantly Layla smiled and went right into my arms. I could have held her for hours, I was so happy to see her and she was indescribably adorable. I'm not just saying this because she's my child, but she was the most amazing baby. I took Layla into the house and then we began setting her room up. I then bathed her and fed her as we watched cartoons and looked at books. I would even try to sing to her, everything I did should have come effortlessly, but sadly, it did not. The hostility within me kept me from being what I wanted to be for her. I would form great thoughts, but when it came time to do it I just couldn't. In the back of my mind, I had a haunting reminder that I would soon be going to prison and have to leave Layla again. I wasn't doing anything to genuinely benefit my daughter, but still I didn't want to go.

My poor daughter—she was taken from her mother and then once again the stranger that everyone seems to call Daddy is leaving again. I had stopped using opiates, but was going through intense withdrawals. Instead I was using Xanax or whatever else I could to curb my anxieties, or allow me to sleep. I was even abusing Benadryl and Tylenol PM. These over-the-counter medications became almost like a narcotic for me. One afternoon after quite some time, Layla's mom and I spoke. We agreed to meet and take Layla shopping. Once again I would have no money, but was expecting a check from Nashville. My mother would see to it that I had money, so we picked up Layla's mom then went to Walmart. All types of thoughts and emotions were running through my head. At that time I hadn't resolved my feelings for Layla's mom. By the time we got into the store Layla went wild with energy. She was intensely happy! We bought her some shoes, some toys, and clothes. Layla got the most joy out of getting a little foam couch, that unfolded into a bed. It had Dora the Explorer on it, one of her favorite cartoons to watch.

After shopping then dropping Layla's mom off, I was heart-broken as we drove away. I looked at Layla through the rearview mirror, and she was just as happy as she could be. I didn't know how to cope with what I was feeling inside, I pretty much demanded that my mother and I stop off at a tavern for some drinks. My mom suggested that we pick up some alcohol and take it home. In my self-centeredness and wanting instant gratification, I coerced her into stopping at the bar she worked for part-time. I didn't even care that Layla was with us. What had I become to be so despicable? We went inside and put Layla into a high chair, and then my mother ordered her a hot dog with fries. We ordered her a sippy cup of milk while I ordered a beer. I instantly slammed it down the hatch, then demanded another. I couldn't stop. I wanted to drink and drink some more until I became numb. We eventually left the bar, and Layla was tired.

My mom was mentally exhausted and said to me, "Look, I'm going out for a while, and you are going to have to hold it together!"

I thought I could, but as soon as my mom left, Layla freaked out. I didn't know what to do other than call Layla's mom. She knew that I had been drinking as soon as she heard my voice, so she came to pick up the baby and then took her over to her mom's house.

After this incident, my days had become numbered. I was constantly reminded that I needed to turn myself into the authorities. Before I did, I remember the last moments I got to spend with Layla before going to prison. Layla fell asleep fairly early the night before. I watched her sleeping in her crib. I'm surprised she didn't wake up from my crying and the tears falling on her. I left her little room, and then went to try and get some rest on the couch. I slept very lightly just in case she would wake up and I could tend to her. At about 8:30 a.m., I heard her in her crib moving around and making noises. I went into the room, and she became one huge smile.

I changed her diaper and made her a bottle of fresh milk, along with a little bowl of cereal snacks. She had to follow every move I made, so we let the dogs outside then went back into the living room and watched some cartoons. I was still very tired, so I lay down on the couch and watched her eat as she danced to silly cartoon music.

She was so cute she would keep looking back at me and just smile. I would say, "I love you, Layla!" And she would just grin. Layla wasn't very affectionate toward me when it came to giving hugs and kisses. She would run off as I would try to cuddle with her. But on this morning, she took a sip of her milk and another bite of cereal. She then climbed up on the couch and lay on my chest. She wrapped her little arms around my neck and lay like that for the longest time.

This was what I so desperately yearned for, and at the same time, I was torn apart because I would have to leave her soon. We lay there together watching cartoons for quite a while. She would leave later that day to go to Layla's other grandmother's home. And then I would face the music, and go to turn myself in at the Montgomery County Jail. I really don't know how I turned myself in on my own. But I did. It was probably the most responsible choice I had ever made in my adult life. I knew that in order to be the dad that Layla so rightfully deserved, I had to do it and embrace change. While looking at my little girl through glass at a visit, I knew it would be the last time I would see her for a very long time. I stayed in County lockup for twenty-one days and then went to the Corrections Reception Center. I never got a visit with Layla. I had only one photo of her. I heard her little voice on the phone only once. I would lay awake on my bunk all hours of the night thinking about her and beating myself up for all the mistakes I had made.

When I had finally surrendered and dedicated my life to following Christ, I was given the strength to cope with missing her. My focus and thoughts became that of taking her to church, teaching her sports, and helping her with her homework. I just wanted to be that solid man she could depend on in any situation. It was important for me to want her to know and love me, but it became more of an importance to let her know that she has a father in heaven who is more important than anything and anyone else.

This chapter was written on Father's Day, June 19, 2011. The last Father's Day I would have to spend away from Layla Grace. By the amazing grace that saved a wretch like me, I was able to recognize the true love the Father has for his child. And the love I would share with my amazing Layla Grace.

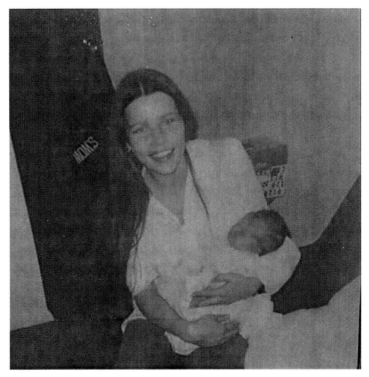

My Mother and I as a Newborn

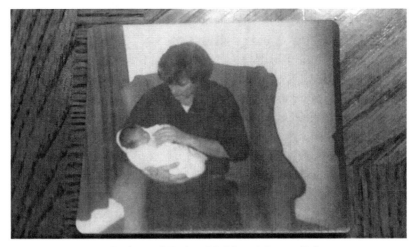

My Biological Father Holding Me as a Baby

My Little Sister Rene 11/23/83 - 7/31/04

My Aunt who tragically took her own life

Layla, My Mom and I on Mothers Day

Noah Henson and I in Nashville TN

My Harley Davidson I named the 'Angel of Mercy'

At a Recovery Event for 'Harley's Against Heroin' 8/12/17

This Little Light of Mine, I'm Gonna Let it Shine

The Devil's Trophy Case
Part I

I had been to prison before, my first number was 616-844. I did seven months and after being released I was taken to the Greyhound bus station. I immediately went to the nearest convenience store and purchased alcohol and cigarettes. I even purchased crack cocaine and smoked it in the parking lot behind a church. While drinking my booze from a Styrofoam cup, I noticed a man laying asleep on the floor. I went outside to have a smoke, and the man who was asleep on the floor had gotten up, stumbled outside, and asked for a light. We both looked at each other in curiosity, he asked me my name and I said, "Johnny Baxter." He then gave me a tainted smile, and said, "Dude, I saved your life!" I knew this guy from overdosing at his house. No he did not save my life! I recall being on the front porch while paramedics frantically worked on me. They would revive me and I would continue to stop breathing. I was in and out of consciousness, I remember saying to one of the paramedics, "Please let me die!" The devil wanted me, but God would not allow it! I was taken to the hospital, and held for observation.

Eventually I was released and I would continue shooting heroin. It didn't take long for me to end back up in jail, then out of jail and into rehab. I would violate the terms and conditions of my probation that led into me going to prison for seven months. And here I was on the day of my release standing face-to-face with an addict I used to get high with. Only having been at the bus station for about an hour, I had a needle in my arm. Six months later I was back in jail, and was on my way to become a prized possession in the Devil's Trophy Case, to return as number 636-824.

Many would say, that this was all the work of the devil. However God had a plan, and paid the ransom for my salvation. I was sentenced to two years in London Correctional Institution. While on the prison bus, I met a man who glorified the life of being a convict. He would say, "Man stick with me, we've got about the same amount of time, so we can get some tattoos, eat and work out together." He said, "Don't worry about a thing man, I've got your back." He prided himself on being a hooch maker, he claimed that would be our ticket to survival. Hooch is a rotgut form of wine made from bread, rotten fruit and sugar.

I arrived at LoCI on September 28, 2010. I wasn't sure who I should be, or how I should carry myself. It was still slightly warm out, so after receiving our housing instructions; we went to the yard to work out. While working out I noticed that the guy I was on the bus with had huge crosses tattooed all over his body. He also had a lot of evil ones too. I asked the guy about the crosses and he said to me, "They're protection for when I die." Now I knew how to be saved, yet I still asked him, "Protection from who?"

He responded, "From God and the devil!" This man actually believed that when he died he would lay in the grave, and because he had some tattoos he would not have to spend an eternity anywhere.

He even thought that he would rise out of the grave, on his own. I wanted to tell him the truth, but I refrained because I didn't want to be that hypocrite preaching Jesus in prison. The man said he saw demons on a regular basis, he also said that he was on heavy psychotropic medications. It didn't take long after my associating with him, that I could sense the evil all around him. God was preparing me for something, and I didn't even know it yet.

One day I saw the same guy making a weapon, the weapon was a shank. A shank is any object that can be forged for the use of stabbing someone. He was acting demonically driven, while making the weapon. I said, "Man, what are you doing?"

And he responded, "Someone is a threat to my hooch operation, so I gotta take them out!" I thought to myself, "Dear God this man has lost his mind!" I thought he was going to stab someone, but instead he planted the shank under another man's mattress. He then had one of his associates drop a note on the (CO's) corrections officer's desk. Within a matter of moments the door was filled with officers surrounding the area, while taking the proclaimed threat away in handcuffs. I felt bad for this man, he was looking at a serious charge and possibly more time. In prison you were forced to live by a different set of codes and belief systems. Being labeled a snitch is very dangerous! A snitch is someone that tries to earn kudos and rewards by reporting criminal behavior. I turned a blind eye to what I saw, and continued minding my own business. I stopped hanging out with the hooch maker, I tried to stay to myself and find peace within my thoughts.

But there is no rest for the wicked. I had destroyed everything that was worthy of having on the outside of the razor wire. I had the appearance of a really mean guy, or at least many have told me, but the truth is, I'm a pretty nice guy that only looks intimidating. Because of my countenance, I was approached by white supremacy gangs. I was approached often. I would tell them, I'd consider hanging out with them, but never would. They were pretty persistent, so one afternoon I agreed to work out with one of the gang members. I explained to him that I wanted to feel accepted and be a part of something.

I wanted someone to genuinely care about me and help me through my problems. The gang member acted as if he were listening, while scanning the yard, worried about what everybody else was doing. He said that by joining their gang I would have to fight, show loyalty and respect. This guy had a huge Nazi symbol on his chest. I wasn't prejudice, nor did I believe in anything that they stood for. The black guys who I had conversations with from time to time saw me associating with the gang members and withdrew from me. I was housed in a very animalistic dorm, and it was hard for me to seek sanity from the noises of late night dice games and people drunk off of hooch. Sometimes I would hear that small voice and it was God saying, "Johnny, I'm waiting."

Periodically I would attend A.A and N.A meetings. I knew without a doubt that I had a drug problem, so I signed up to join a program called the Renaissance. It was a residential drug treatment within the prison compound. God had convicted my spirit to stay away from the white supremacy gang. I would still be approached by them on the yard and in the chow hall. I would always make up an excuse as to why I wouldn't hang out with them. While coming out of a NA meeting, I saw the appointed leader of the gang who was trying to recruit me.

He came up to me and said, "How ya been bro? I've been in medical isolation, so I'm wondering whom I'm gonna have to fight?"

I told him I've been staying to myself and said, "Take care of yourself and God Bless you." It wasn't long after me saying that to him, he was severely beaten up by his own gang members. I knew right away that prison gangs were nothing to mess with.

I would still hear that small voice from God saying, "Johnny, who are you going to turn to?"

I could see all the evidence and that there was no way to run from him, but I still wasn't ready to surrender. Everything outside of the brick, concrete and razor wire were all in shambles. Everything inside of me spiritually, was broken and felt beyond repair. I attempted to call my mother one afternoon, as I finished entering the numbers into the phone it would only ring once.

The recorded message would say that the number I was trying to reach had been disconnected. My heart sank and I was crushed, I felt completely alone. Or so I thought? There was only one way to go, God had shown me the signs my entire existence and I always ran the other way. The devil had stripped me of everything. I had no foundation, all I had was a deep dark basement! A flood of tears began to fall from my eyes, I carried what little dignity and myself over to my bunk area. I climbed into my bunk and pulled the state issued sheet over my head. I was weeping to the point it was hard to breathe. I didn't care who saw me that way, I didn't care about carrying the tough persona. I was broken and in need of repair.

I cried out to God and said, "I have failed you miserably. I can no longer do this on my own. I need you to show me how to live and I will follow you the rest of my days!" In that moment the most perfect peace came over me and I felt as though I was a child wrapped in swaddling clothes. The tears had stopped, and I just lay there feeling the powerful presence and love of Jesus Christ. My mind became filled with pleasant thoughts, these were not my thoughts, but the thoughts the Holy Spirit had instilled in me. My feelings of failure had dissipated and now turned into hope.

I no longer felt fear but now felt strength. I continued to lie there, in awe of God's presence all around me. Suddenly a sharp pain began in my right ear. It hurt so bad that it nearly brought me back to tears. I could hear God's peaceful voice saying, "Be still and know that I am God." The pressure was back and forth from my ear, it was almost like a vacuum was sucking something out of it. But that something did not want to leave. I know now that it was God removing that evil spirit of addiction that had plagued me for nearly twenty years. The pain continued for hours, almost to the point I was ready to go to the infirmary. But God would still speak into my spirit and say, "Be still, my son." So I did as he told me to do.

Eventually the pain subsided, and I was in a place of peace again. I felt almost absent from my body and present with the Lord. It was the most amazing experience that I have ever had in my life or will have in my life. No longer would I ever doubt the power of Jesus Christ! I was able to rest that night and I had become someone new overnight! The very next day as soon as I was able to enter the chapel, I did. I went in, got on my knees and prayed. Tears began to fall. I attended a service and my spirit hungered to know the Word of God. During the service I looked around within the chapel and noticed a black man who appeared to be in perfect peace while praising God. It just so happened he was housed in the same dorm that I was, so that evening after service I approached him and introduced myself. I gave him a very brief testimony and said I was interested in knowing the Word of God and singing in the chapel choir.

He proceeded to tell me that after 9:00 p.m. count, he and some other Christian brothers gathered together to have a Bible study in the day area. He said I was more than welcome to attend, so I said I would join them. I had never really tried to read the Bible, I wasn't even really sure where to turn to find the books. But I continued to go every night to study with those brothers and grow with God! My situation reminds me of Proverbs 22:6: Train up a child in the way they should go and when they are old they shall not depart from it.

God had brought me back from death and into life. I would spend a lot of time with my brother who was on fire for the Lord. He would give me various books to read: books on deliverance, spiritual warfare, and the power of prayer. My eyes began to open as to where I really was, and what was really going on around me. I was letting go of my worldly ways, I was on fire to live for Jesus Christ! One night I was under a heavy spiritual attack.

I went to Bible study, and there was a brother in our group who was very mysterious. He didn't show any emotions, and when he would read the Word of God; he really didn't seem connected to it. I verbally attacked this man, accusing him to be all knowing about the Bible, but not being able to live it. Later I would find out the reason he was in prison was for stealing money from his church. Apparently he was a trusted individual and an elder, filling his own bank account with money that was supposed to be used to help the community.

I felt bad for having judged him. And who was I to think I was holier than thou, by newly dedicating my life to Christ? I asked my Bible study group to pray over me, and so they did. I felt instant relief but would continue to feel the pains of growing as a Christian. My life was changing, I had indescribable joy. I read the Bible every day, and when I did it touched me in ways that empowered my spirit. I would join the chapel choir. God had given back my dreams, hopes, and aspirations. I didn't worry so much about life outside of the razor wire, I was ready to become a better me. I would stay in the chaotic dorm awaiting to join the Renaissance program. One day I was passing the hooch maker I met on the prison bus.

I simply said to him, "God bless you." I could see that it angered him. On the yard, or going to chow, I would see the gang members who had tried to enlist me. They would still approach me and ask if I was going to kick it (hang out)? I simply would say, "No, thanks, guys, I'm going to church and working out with Jesus." They would respond by saying they were a church. I would continue about my business and keep it moving. God always had a way of keeping me moving in the midst of evil and its snares. I was being renewed and transformed. I would pray from my heart, to feel compassion for others.

While at choir practice, I was talking to a brother in the chapel. He said to me, "Johnny, you have one of the most amazing voices, it is powerful and when I hear you sing. I feel the Holy Spirit." I humbled myself, as he continued to say, "God is going to put a calling on your life, Johnny, right now you may be in the devil's trophy case, but you are no longer valuable to the devil." I thought a lot about what he said and this revelation, was revealed to me. There were about 2,700 prisoners in London Correctional. All were convicted of charges ranging from theft, drugs, assault, rape and murder. All were trophies of the devil. Inside of this trophy case, demonic forces were at work to ornament and polish the ultimate hell bound soul. I knew that when I gave my life to Christ, that I would just be collecting dust in the devil's trophy case. I was no longer a prize to him. I began to think of every inmate as a trophy, but what was written on their placard? I could only imagine God removing me from the trophy case, then polishing me and removing the placard the devil had placed on me. My placard would now read "Soul winner for Christ."

I was finally moved out of the chaotic dorm and placed into the Renaissance dorm for the drug program. I felt that it was where God intended me to be. The program began in January. Immediately after my starting the program, everyone knew how I felt for Jesus. Everything that I would share while speaking, would correlate with how I felt about God and his will in my life. In drug treatment they express the importance of knowing a higher power.

The twelve steps of any recovery fellowship are designed to bring you closer to God. The twelve steps themselves, are biblically inspired. But as a universal approach, rather than putting the name of Jesus on them; they say to believe in a power greater than yourself. My neighbor in the dorm was a Muslim. He explained to me that he once was a Christian. He claimed to have found the truth, and offered me some literature involving contradictions of the Bible. I read it, but didn't buy into it. In Jesus's own words he said, "To love our neighbors, as ourselves." I didn't have any ill feelings toward him or his belief, because that was something he would one day take up with God. I could see the look of disgust in his face, as I would be laying on my bunk reading my Bible. Drawing closer to God, was the only way I was going to make it through. I attended my first group, and the counselor who was a pastor said to me, "I see you love the Lord and that's great, but do not hide behind the Bible."

I wasn't hiding behind the Bible, it was my shield against the fiery darts of the enemy. I was offended by what he had said, so I prayed about it and still believed that I was where God wanted me to be. When I was assigned to my small group, I would have a Muslim counselor who was from the Middle East. I had no reason to dislike her, but I felt as though she didn't want to acknowledge me in our groups. I would face a lot of persecution in prison, I didn't at all consider it ironic. After all, the Bible says in Matthew 10:28: Ye shall be hated of all men for my name sake; but he that endureth to the end shall be saved. A lot of prisoners are angry with God. They want to blame him for their circumstances that led up to them being in prison. Coming from dysfunctional homes, poverty-stricken neighborhoods, and a great deal of misfortune. I had no one to blame other than myself for being in prison. I chose to run with the devil, and had to pay the consequences for it. Two years seemed like a very long road ahead. But it would be enough time for me to walk with Christ and discover my true identity.

The Devil's Trophy Case
Part II

As a part of the Renaissance program, all new clients had to write what was called an "addiction story." It was basically a shorter version of the chapter "Runnin with the Devil" within this book. I was assigned to a mentor who would review the writing of my story; they would also review my approach on other assignments. I did not see eye to eye with the mentor I was assigned to, he was very critical of my story. We finally would come to an agreement, and I was scheduled to read it aloud at our community meeting on January 31, 2011. I prayed fervently the night before, and the morning of. I was experiencing all types of emotions and I wasn't too comfortable with revealing my life story to a bunch of prisoners. I thought they would find my story as a moment of weakness, and then try to take advantage of me. God had reassured me within my spirit that no matter what happened, he would be there. I knew I needed to get the pain out, so I brushed my teeth, combed my hair, put on my state issued uniform and then made my way into the meeting area. It was a beautiful morning, the sun was shining so bright that I could barely see the forty or fifty men, and the staff who sat before me.

After the program coordinator had made his announcements and introduced me, I began to read my story. I was okay at first, until I got to the part where I spoke about the death of my sister. I tried to keep my composure, and carry on reading. I spoke of the intense guilt that I felt about choosing drugs over my daughter. Tears fell that I could no longer hold back, I didn't want these men to see me cry after all I was in prison, and I thought I had to be tough. After finishing my story silence was over the community for what seemed like an eternity. They then applauded, but in that silence I looked out at all the faces while squinting from the blinding sun.

I saw many of them appeared to be angry and through my discernment I felt as though I was about to be verbally attacked. In that moment I felt intense anxiety. It felt as though tight ropes were being wrapped around me, followed by sharp stabbing pains. It even made it hard to breathe. I just stood there as they opened up the floor for comments; prisoners would comment first and then the staff. I already knew what was coming, sure enough I was criticized for my use of the word *demons* and constant mentioning of God.

I was chastised for how I portrayed myself in the Renaissance dorm by being so outspoken about my faith. I was not bitter or offended by it, because like I said, I expected it. I figured that when the staff would comment, they would acknowledge my roots of addiction and not comment on my faith. My small group counselor, the Muslim woman; got up and literally started yelling at me. I don't remember exactly what she said, but the thing that stood out the most was when she said, "What you believe in Mr. Baxter, is not of God!" She inadvertently attacked my belief in Jesus Christ. My God was more than a prophet unlike what the nation of Islam chooses to believe about him. I started to become angry, but remained silent. The last person to comment was the program coordinator.

He said to me, "How do you feel?"

I responded, "Attacked!"

The program coordinator knew that I had stopped taking my psych meds. After exposing me as being mentally ill, he then would also start in on my faith. He said that I didn't need to hide behind God, and that if I continued to do so I would not recover. In the back of my mind I used the Word of God as an affirmation. Philippians 4:13: I can do all things through Christ who strengtheneth me. Now don't get me wrong, some of this feedback was constructive and I was able to receive it. But as they continued to poke and prod about my belief in Jesus, I would get angrier.

The program coordinator smiled and said, "You're mad aren't you?"

Instantly I said, "Yes!" I told them how I really felt, and when it was all said and done I went back to my bunk feeling completely torn apart. I stopped being so outspoken in the dorm, I continued to pray that God revealed to me whether I should continue in the Renaissance program? I would go to group and sense the overwhelming tension between my Muslim counselor and me. I continued to keep quiet in groups and would share my feelings only in the chapel and AA/NA meetings. God continued to remind me I was not alone and still blessed me with the strength to persevere. I always found peace while in the chapel, singing and praising God. I started leading the choir on several occasions. I would lead worship in different genres of Christian music. Whether it was Rock, R+B or Gospel I would find joy in singing about the Lord.

In the book of Isaiah 61:3, it is mentioned, "Put on the garment of praise for the spirit of heaviness." And let me tell you, that heaviness would leave every time I sang for Jesus! It was such a blessing to be able to witness such a variety of different services. I didn't get caught up or lost in one form of doctrine. I just wanted to hear the news about Jesus and feel the movement of the Holy Spirit. Some services were absolutely on Holy Fire! I felt as though I could have lived in the chapel, but constantly I had to be reminded; I was in the devil's trophy case.

Some days I felt like I was going to snap, especially when it seemed like the prison and its staff were over exerting their authority. But God would show up with a blessing to diffuse my anger. As the days continued to pass I stayed focused on studying the Bible. I began working on tests to become ordained. I would continue to battle my own emotions in the Renaissance program. Another way I found release, was by starting to work out. Not only did I want to exercise my body, but I wanted to strengthen my mind and spirit. I started out running, something I despised doing.

Although I was a master at running from my problems. I decided to challenge myself, and push myself to the limit. I started out running a couple of laps at a time around the track. In a short amount of time I had gotten up to four miles and was able to do one thousand push-ups. I'm not trying to boast, I'm only saying that Christ gave me the strength to do things I never thought were possible. I would envision Jesus and my sister smiling at the final turn of each lap. I would also envision my little Layla in a futuristic sense, riding her bicycle next to me. Before entering the devil's trophy case I was not active at all, sometimes I would sleep up to sixteen hours a day. I smoked anywhere from one to three packs of cigarettes a day. But now, the gospel was being fulfilled in my life. In 2 Corinthians 5:17, the apostle Paul wrote, "Therefore if any man be in Christ, he is a new creature; old things are passed away: behold, all things are becoming new."

I never felt so alive, and although I had an idea of God's purpose for my life, it would start to become more evident when I sang in the chapel. Prisoners that I had never spoken to, or fellowship with would come up to me and say that my singing moved them spiritually. I remember looking out at the congregation one time, and a brother was in tears as I sang "Mighty to Save." Another brother would say that he had a vision of me holding my hands up in praise to God, long after I left the pulpit area.

I would humbly say to these men and guests, "Thanks, but it's not about me. I'm just the vessel, it's all about Jesus!" Sure, I was singing, but the Holy Spirit did all the work. The one major problem of being a Christian in prison, was that other people who professed to be believers were quick to point out my flaws and shortcomings. The same people who professed to be believers, would engage in gambling, pornography, have a foul mouth, and were gang affiliated. I don't say this to be judgmental, I'm only saying this because it's hard to accept someone's opinion of you when they are not honoring God with their behaviors. This type of criticism forced me into isolation. Isolating yourself is how the devil plays tricks with your mind.

Before I truly found Jesus, I was always in fear of being alone. I had to rely on everyone else for everything, whether it was material or emotional. I couldn't stand being alone because the devil and I had created such a hostile place within my thoughts. But when Jesus entered my life, never again would I feel alone. I could have been in prison on a desolate island by myself, and been completely content. Staying to myself and focusing on the Lord, I was able to avoid a lot of conflicting situations. I pretty much did everything alone. I was no longer approached by gang members, they didn't even acknowledge me when they would see me on the yard. When being processed at the Corrections Reception Center, you are forced to get your head shaved, so you are recognized on your inmate ID. I didn't want to look anything like a white supremacist.

They had the typical look: bald heads and a goatee. I began growing my hair out very long. I couldn't help but see so many lost souls on that compound. I grieved the thoughts about how many of them would go to hell because they refused to acknowledge God. It was a shame being that they were in a living hell already, being in prison. In passing on the yard, I would hear the same guys talking about the same things.

Sometimes it was for months, and eventually it would lead up to a year. Conversations about how much drugs they would do, how they had a connection set up outside to plan a robbery and get paid. They thought money was the only way they could start over. But what exactly were they starting over? It's obvious they were starting another trip right back into the devil's trophy case. I still would continue to try witnessing to those I thought God had appointed.

Prison has to be one of the hardest places to share the gospel with someone. Most prisoners carried the mentality I once did, they thought finding God in prison was hypocritical. My outlook on that had completely changed, after having had a spiritual awakening. Some folks were receptive, I would ask if they needed prayer and would even hold small Bible studies within my bunk area. It really blew my mind to hear that prayers were being answered for those men and their families. I was genuinely happy for them, but at the same time it was a haunting reminder of feeling forsaken by my own family.

I wrote my grandmother. I even sent a package with some Christian books. I also wrote my grandfather, who is a man of God; I figured if I were to hear from anyone, it would have been from him. At 2:45 p.m., on most days, the mail list would be posted. I would be so hopeful to see my name on it, eagerly hoping for a picture or news about Layla. Every day was a disappointment; I had to be reminded of who I was before I went to prison.

I eventually became numb to it. I thank God I had one true friend I could depend on! My best friend in Virginia would always send a card once a month, and enough money for me to moderately survive. She was such a huge blessing, I don't know how my needs would've been met without her support? We would talk on the phone every once in a while, and I would feel helpless to hear about her deteriorating health. Some days it felt as though the cross that I must carry was too heavy to bear.

I would try to confide in my group members of the Renaissance program. I would never walk away feeling any better about myself. I would genuinely just try to let them know that even though I was Christian; I was also a human being trying to cope with many struggles. Somehow it always seemed to turn into the persecution of Johnny the Christian. Or the question would be raised, "Are you complying with your mental health?" Only by the grace of God I was able to graduate the first phase of the Renaissance program. It was a learning experience, and I did gain some very valuable tools to help me in my recovery. I also was able to develop an understanding with my Muslim counselor. I could still sense tension but we remained respectful toward each other. She would reveal some things about her life to our group that softened the hard part of my heart I had toward her. I was also able to graduate several different programs, such as anger management, keys to a loving relationship, and a twelve-step program.

On Wednesday, April 13, 2011, I turned thirty-two years old. I was blessed to receive mail from all three of my best friend's sons. Those boys had seen me at my absolute worst, and in the grips of my addiction I would steal and sell their things for drugs. I couldn't believe that a family could love me so much after all I had done to them. They never turned their backs on me, even after I had wronged them more than my own family. I think the only explanation for them continuing to support me, was that they were a Christian family. I also would receive a card from my grandfather. To me the card seemed as if he forced himself to send it. Maybe he just didn't know what to say, because he really didn't say anything in it at all. There was a very little note inside, simply telling me to abide in my time during my walk with Jesus. So I continued to do just that. As the week of the passion approached I became very excited. We had been rehearsing in the chapel for an Easter Cantata entitled "He Chose the Nails."

The choir director asked if I would sing a song called "Thief." It was a song sung from the perspective of one of the men who would be crucified with Jesus. Pleading before Christ to remember him. It was a very powerful song, and I considered it an honor to be able to sing it. We performed on the Passover, just one week after my birthday.

We made three crosses out of cardboard. As the intro music began to play for "Thief," we walked up to the crosses and stood before them, holding our arms out as if being crucified. Something about that song allowed me to feel like I was actually on Golgotha. One of my close Christian brothers would portray Jesus and he began to cry during the song. I looked out among the congregation, some men were crying while others were on their knees in submission to the Lord. I would've never believed after playing rock 'n' roll music in front of large crowds, that I would feel more accomplished and purpose driven as I did during that Easter Cantata.

When the praises go up, the blessings come down. I soon would discover that I was eligible for a transitional control release. If the judge allowed it, I could possibly leave prison sometime in November 2011. I prayed and prayed about it. I asked God that if it was according to his will please let it be done.

The Devil's Trophy Case
Part III

In early May, I started the continuing care phase of the Renaissance program. I was very skeptical about doing so, I became more interested in moving out of the dorm and into the spiritual dorm to fellowship with my Christian brothers. I still liked the idea of receiving one good day a month off of my sentence for being in the Renaissance program. I figured I owed it to Layla, and I knew there was so much more to learn about recovery. My new group counselor was an attractive black female that professed to be a Christian. I could tell right away, that she had an inferiority complex, as well as ego issues. I figured it would be just a matter of time before I would be terminated from the program. But I figured I would ride the wave until I fell off, just hoping to make it to the shore. I stopped sharing in groups, I no longer could handle the persecution from others too well. I avoided conflict by remaining silent, or only speaking when I was asked. I would still regularly attend AA/NA meetings, and did all that was expected of me concerning my assignments. Up until this point I was hungry to be a part of the Renaissance program. I became confused whether it was God's will or my own will to stay in the program?

During one group session, I shared about a conflict between my bunkie and I. I was angry about something and felt the group would be the place to vent. I discovered that someone in my group who was a friend of my bunkie, had a problem with me for quite some time. This guy was supposedly a reformed prison gang member, who came from another institution. He verbalized that he hadn't liked the fact I was asked to put my Bible down in treatment and never did.

Words were exchanged that almost led into us fighting. Truth be told I was a little scared because this guy was huge, and he probably would have cleaned my clock. We ended up resolving our issues and continued in our group. In the latter part of the treatment I began to focus on what I thought were all the negative aspects of the Renaissance program, I was told that this was common addict behavior. I began to wake up feeling very angry, some days it felt much like the times I used to get high. I diligently continued to seek the Lord, but I wasn't exactly the compassionate Christian that I could be. Everyone seemed to notice, and it gave them a reason to label me Johnny the Christian hypocrite. I even started to become complacent in the chapel choir.

All the bickering and control issues, began to take its toll on me. I still had a chip on my shoulder, with the attitude of doing what I wanted to do, and when I wanted to do it. That attitude would cause more turmoil for me in Renaissance program. In June 2011, it was our dorm's commissary day I was supposed to be in group, but chose to go get my things from the store. I knew that there would be consequences. After shopping I unloaded my things and secured them in my footlocker. The CO then called for me, I already knew what was coming. My counselor wanted to see me, so I went to recovery services, and sat among all the staff to discuss what I had done. I didn't tried to justify things, because I couldn't. They asked me what type of punishment I thought should be instituted? I replied, I really don't know?

They said they would discuss what to do, and then sent me back to the dorm. The next day I sat with them again, and was told that I was being written a ticket for being out of place. I was also told that I would need to sweep and mop the group rooms, for a period of thirty days. Cleaning was to start the very next day. The next day I was in a Dual Recovery Anonymous meeting, rather than waiting on my counselor to return from lunch and receive her instructions. My counselor was infuriated, she grabbed the program coordinator, removed me from the meeting and asked me to sit in another group room. The big guy who I once had a problem with, tried to intervene on my behalf. She snapped at him and told him to mind his own business. In the end we were both terminated from the Renaissance program. I was angry and hurt, I was only three weeks away from graduating the entire program. Now I had lost out on one good day a month, off of my sentence. That was not my sole intention for joining the program, I genuinely wanted to learn about my addiction and how to recover. I knew it wouldn't be long, and I would be moved out of the Renaissance dorm. I went to plead my case before the program coordinator in hopes that he would allow me, to stay housed in the dorm. I had become accustomed and comfortable in that quiet dorm, I did not want to go back to a place of chaos. He then said, "John I already have you placed on a move sheet and you will be swapping beds with someone from the C2 dorm." That place felt like hell to me.

My anger and resentments toward the Renaissance program really piqued at this point. I would ask God, Why? It all felt as though I was stepping backward. Once again I would be in the midst of gambling and alcohol. I was about eight months clean and sober, it felt as though I was Daniel in the Bible and was being thrown into the lions den.

June of 2011, I was moved back into the "flames of hell." As I entered the dorm, I was overwhelmed with the stench of cigarette smoke. I unpacked my things and would try to get comfortable. Immediately my neighbors would start rolling up cigarettes, and asked me if I smoked?

I said no, and then they asked, "Are you a snitch?"

After some time, my anger and resentment made it hard to withstand wanting to smoke. I eventually gave into the temptation and started smoking again. I became ashamed of myself, God had delivered me from this and I was letting him down. But what I was most ashamed about was that Bible pages were used for rolling papers. Here I am supposed to be this devout Christian, and I'm smoking the Bible as a cigarette. I felt like I was falling away, I began acting the same way for tobacco as I did for drugs and alcohol on the streets. It sounds crazy, but the activities and hustle associated with a bag of tobacco in prison were the same as copping dope in an abandoned crackhouse.

People began to mock me, and I pretty much gave them every opportunity to do so. I knew this wasn't who I wanted to be, I knew deep down I had to let the cigarettes go. God was convicting my spirit while at the same time the devil always appeared with temptation. I went through money that I didn't even have, I neglected the food I needed only to buy cigarettes. In prison a cigarette was anywhere from three to five dollars. As you can imagine, in prison, it's a very expensive habit to maintain.

One day I would go back to recovery services and put myself at the mercy of the program coordinator. I begged for him to allow me back into the Renaissance program. I didn't like the idea of failing at anything. He told me that it would be some time before I could enter back in. First Corinthians 10:13 says, "There hath no temptation taken you such as common to man but God is faithful, who will not suffer you to be tempted above that ye are able, but will with temptation also make away to escape." I began to meditate on this scripture and allowed it to rekindle my desire to quit smoking. I then put my faith into action, I stepped up my recovery meeting attendance. I exposed my guilt, shame, anger and resentments. I then started reducing the amount of cigarettes I smoked. I continually sought the Lord through prayer, while exercising as much as I could.

God soon provided a way out, another turn at the intersection in my spiritual journey. I sacrificed a comfortable bottom bunk, for a top bunk located in the spiritual dorm across the hall. I continued to pray that God would allow me to leave prison altogether, in hopes of getting a transitional control release. But it was overruled by the judge. I wasn't really ready to leave prison yet. God would still need to hold, shape and condition me for a life in the free world. I didn't stop smoking altogether right away, but after two weeks of living in the spiritual dorm I gave that burden to Jesus. Once again he would take away the desire, and placed me on a path of reconciliation.

The Devil's Trophy Case
Part IV

I didn't really know what to expect moving into the spiritual dorm. There were a lot of rumors surrounding about what went on in that dorm. I just knew that I was slipping back into old patterns, and I needed to seek the Lord, through fellowship in a less chaotic environment. My bunkie was in his late fifties and had done almost thirty years in prison. He was convicted of a heinous crime, and was probably never going home. It was easy to tell that even though he lived in a spiritual dorm, he had lost faith. I thought he and I would bump heads, so I stayed out of my bunk area most of the time. My drive to workout became very intense, actually because I have an addictive personality; I went overboard with it. Relaxation, balance, and moderation had never really been something I was good at practicing. I think it had gotten better, but still had a long way to go.

At nights I would dive into the Bible while looking at the photo of Layla I had taped inside of it. It was all I could do to pray that she was happy, and that she was getting all that she deserved. I got involved with prayer shares in the day area, it was a great way to fellowship with brothers who were on fire for Christ. Some were a little self-righteous, and it had been my experience that many Christians were capable of being that way. Especially new believers, Lord knows I thought I was holier than thou, maybe that's why I had to slip up, and have a reality slap in the face.

I began to feel like I was headed into a very good place during my walk with Jesus. I stopped judging others so harshly. But when someone would inform me of a certain prisoner's conviction, I couldn't help but feel disgusted and angry. Most of the time someone would say, "Man that dude you were just talking to is a child molester." Or they would say he was a rapist. My initial reaction was to form an opinion and distance myself from them. I was the father of a little girl, and I would protect my child's innocence at all costs.

I earnestly had to pray for the understanding, that even though these men had committed these terrible crimes; they were still children of God. They also were serving out their punishment, so what gave me the right to punish them as well? Other prisoners did, I witnessed men lying in pools of blood by assaults, when another prisoner became disturbed by their charges. For some reason the spiritual dorm was filled particularly, with men who had committed sex crimes. They hid in the dorm, and it was pathetic to see the reputation the dorm had gotten. London Correctional was in need of a major movement toward Christ.

As mid-September approached, my best friend scheduled a visit, it would be the one and only visit I would have in prison. The last visit I had was when my mother brought Layla to the Montgomery County Jail; I literally only saw her for four minutes. I was so excited to be getting a visit, I hadn't seen my best friend in two years. She was coming up from Virginia and would be bringing two of her sons. I felt the spiritual warfare, one afternoon just three days prior to my visit; my bunkie and I had an altercation. He called me an explicit name that in prison would only equal into a fight. He said that he didn't care about my visit or my life, for the first time in prison I was ready to lash out in physical violence. But for the first time in my life, I thought before reacting. My pride was ripping me apart, but I swallowed it back and removed myself from near him. I wasn't going to let the devil steal my blessing like he had so many times.

Instead, I prayed for my bunkie, I prayed that God would bless him. I knew he was spiritually broken, I couldn't imagine doing all that time, with no hope of going home. But I continued to pray that God would reveal himself to him, and he would feel inner joy and peace. After a couple days I spoke with the dorm staff and asked if either he or I could be moved. It became uncomfortable to share space with him, and I truly hadn't let go of my resentment. I wanted to beat him up, for disrespecting me and calling me a harsh word. That would've been a representation of the old Johnny, I always thought by using my fists that would solve the problem. The truth about that, is it cost me my freedom on more than one occasion. My bunkie was moved, however in the process I upset the prisoner who was the sergeant's clerk.

Shortly thereafter, I was moved out of the spiritual dorm. I had been moved to a different dorm for the fifth time. This time I embraced it, and said, "God put me where you want me to be."

I ended up in the B2 dorm; it wasn't all that bad or nearly as chaotic as the other dorms I had been in. Sure there were still people smoking cigarettes and marijuana, and being taken to the hole for being drunk. None of that mattered, because the Lord kept me in a good place mentally. My neighbors would light up a cigarette, and the temptation to smoke was gone. I started becoming more balanced with my biblical studies, meeting attendance, and working out.

Around the same time, I took a break from the chapel choir. It became overwhelming to me, there was a lot of internal conflict among the other members. We were still doing a lot of the same material, I told the worship leader that I would be back as soon as we started the Christmas rehearsals in October. He was a little disappointed, I could see it in his face. There were other brothers disheartened by my absence as well. I assured them all, that it was only a break. Days later, I would get some medical news that would cause me to worry. I felt that I needed to try and write my mother again. I had a chest x-ray that showed spots on my lungs.

I had lost a lot of weight and was actually the smallest I had ever been: 5'8" and 172 lbs. Even though this medical issue raised concerns, I felt more healthy than what I did at fifteen years old. I wrote my mom a letter, she wrote me back; the letter was a painful reminder of the monster I once was. She didn't want anything to do with me. It hurt, but not like it always did. I was able to get outside of myself, by witnessing to new Christians. I didn't have to put myself out there like I was some spiritual zealot, I think my light just began to shine a little brighter. We fellowshipped and studied the Word, and I even introduced them to some of my workout routines. This was something I normally did alone. God continued to do amazing things within London Correctional Institution.

One day the guy who was trying to recruit me in joining a prison gang, would approach me. He had seen my passion for Christ for over a year to respect me enough and not ask me to join the gang. I think he just wanted a friend, who was real. Even though I didn't believe or stand for what he was a part of, I had a lot of respect for his ability to be a leader. I felt compelled to witness to him. I thought if this man can apply his leadership toward honoring Christ; he could really have an impact within the prison. I started by making some meals out of what little we were able to buy from the commissary. Everything was made with ramen noodles. In prison we call it Breaking. If I had a little extra in food, I would give it to him.

One day he would say, "Johnny, you're a really good dude." Even though it was coming from a prisoner, it allowed me to feel really good about myself. I said to him," Unfortunately, it took me coming to prison to learn how to be a good dude." I also said that God had to sit me down for a while, so I could see just how bad of a monster I had become. A few days later he left for transitional control housing. I prayed that whatever seed I planted in the spiritual sense, would create a desire within him to follow God.

On October 6, 2011, I was having my morning cup of coffee while watching the local news. A segment was aired about a young man from my city, who was wanted in connection of an aggravated robbery. The surveillance video showed him plain as day pointing a gun at a store clerk of a convenience store. For some reason it did not surprise me. This same individual was someone that was recently released from LoCI, he had just left prison and was already on his way back to the devil's trophy case. Now he was looking at some serious time. I started to pray for every man carrying out their sentence, within that compound. Here they were, doing all this time then getting out with no hope of living a productive life in the free world. I saw many people get excited around their release date, only to return with more time than they just had completed. It was all more the reason, for me to follow the Lord and carry out his will on my life. I only had seven months to go. It was time to create a plan of action for my release.

The Devil's Trophy Case
Part V

I had heard many of times during the course of the Renaissance program that "God would save my soul, but recovery would save my butt!" That slogan began to resonate within me, after all if I wasn't able to manage my recovery and made the choice to get high, everything including my walk with Christ would go down the drain. Once again I would humble myself and go to recovery services to speak with the program coordinator. I pled my case before him and said that there was so much more I needed to learn about recovery before I went home.

I vowed that I would do whatever the program suggested, and leave my conversations of faith for the chapel and my prayer time. He agreed to have me back, and placed me on the list to start the program over in three months. I knew that with only seven months to go, before I would leave London Correctional. I needed to get involved with as much programming as I could. I joined a class that went beyond anger management, it was a class on how to prevent domestic violence. I learned a lot about myself during the course of those eight weeks, what my triggers were and what my boundaries would be if I pursued another relationship. I continued to join Bible studies every Sunday morning in the chapel.

I would still sing from time to time in the chapel choir, but the drama continued within it so I wasn't as active as I was once before. I started having an overwhelming feeling of energy, it would bring about fear and anxiety about my going home. I still did not know where I was going to go, I met with a release coordinator and the parole board. Although I would not be on parole, I was sanctioned to what is called post-release control. Basically it was one year of probation that if I violated, I would return to prison to do one year.

When asked where I was going to stay, I didn't have an answer. This brought on a deeper sense of fear and anxiety to the point I started becoming manic. I had stopped taking psych meds, because I knew that only Jesus was the great physician. I ended up going to the hole for two weeks. Apparently I was placed in the hole for making a reference about going home. The CO that was working the graveyard shift overheard me in a conversation. That conversation was taken out of context and they thought I was making a plan to escape. While in the hole my mind ran wild, I was completely isolated with only a Bible. I began flipping out on the guards, throwing my food trays out of the slot. I had no reason to be in the hole, but I knew if I didn't chill out I would compromise getting back into the Renaissance program.

After my second week I was released back to the B2 dorm. I was sanctioned to take my psych meds as prescribed by the doctor, and if I didn't I would be going to the hole again. Every night I would go to the infirmary for pill call, I was given Lithium and Lamictal. After a few days the fear and anxiety began to subside. I called my best friend in Virginia one afternoon, and she informed me that her oldest son was going to allow me to stay with his family, upon my release. I was extremely grateful and overjoyed. Her son who once was a thug, had turned his life around and started living for the Lord. He thought I deserved a fair shot to show everyone I was genuine about the change in my life.

In January I was moved back into the Renaissance dorm, awaiting the next program to start in February. I had forgotten just how peaceful it was to live in that dorm, suddenly the idea of my going home didn't seem so scary. When the program started in February, I was assigned to another female counselor who was a new staff member. I was relieved to know that she was a Christian, however I would keep my vow to be silent about my faith in groups.

I was back at phase 1 within the program, but that didn't matter because recovery is always about the first step. I rewrote and shared my addiction story, this time it was relieving to let it all go. I still had hoped at some point to receive another letter from my Mom with a picture of Layla, but never did. I did my best to stay positive in knowing that I would be seeing her soon. I had gotten so much more out of the Renaissance program this time around. I even began working with a sponsor who had been locked up sober for nearly eight years. I chose him because he was a huge dude, and at one time was a professional boxer. I needed someone to hold me accountable and wasn't scared to tell me like it really was. Up to this point I had not done any step work, most of the Renaissance program curriculum was based out of workbooks.

My sponsor would begin giving me assignments out of the Narcotics Anonymous step working guide. Through this process I was able to really get to the roots of my addiction. It allowed me to really take a look at my part for the unmanageability throughout my life. Every question caused me to write out a detailed description, of what I thought, felt and the consequences of my actions. Steps one through three were relatively easy. I knew that I had a problem with drugs and that my life had become unmanageable. I truly believed that a power greater than myself (Jesus) could restore me to sanity. I had already made the decision to turn my will and life over to the care of God as I understood him. The Bible and my experiences gave a crystal clear vision into my faith. When it came time to work the fourth step that was when the real work had begun. Making a searching and fearless moral inventory of myself. Working this step allowed me to think outside of my addicted mind.

I was able to see the cause of my emotional instability and find the solution in learning a new way to live. I had reached a turning point in my life, I was able to recognize my strengths and assets. After completing the fourth step I was able to sit with my sponsor and review the inventory I had collected. We moved right into the fifth step, where I was able to admit the exact nature of my wrongs. He laid it on me straight and to the point, bringing on an overwhelming sense of clarity. It helped hearing the perspective of my sponsor, because he had an unbiased opinion of my situations. After completing a fifth step, my sponsor notified recovery services that I was ready to share my experience, strength and hope at the Thursday night Narcotics Anonymous meeting. This was the largest meeting, we would have at LoCI.

I was nervous about sharing the innermost details of my life with complete strangers. Before doing so I said a quick prayer asking for God's blessing and that my words would be able to reach someone. I spoke for nearly forty-five minutes, afterward all the prisoners gave me a standing ovation. They encouraged me about maintaining my sobriety after going home. They also said they respected the changes they had seen and to watch me grow during my time at London Correctional Institution. I was able to complete steps one through eight, I was also able to complete once again the first phase of the Renaissance program. This time it had become more meaningful, because it was about my recovery and I had stopped fighting to prove myself.

As the weeks dwindled into days, I truly felt as though I was ready to become a productive member of society. I walked to the yard saying goodbyes to the friends that I had made, I prayed with my brothers in the chapel, and prayed that God would order my steps all the way through that gate and beyond. The night before my release I couldn't sleep at all. All I could do was visualize what life would be like on the other side, of that razor wire. My best friend made plans to be in Ohio, to pick me up with her son. At 6:00 a.m. I eagerly sat at the edge of my bunk after giving away my hygiene and things I had collected over the last eighteen months. My name was called by the CO to report to receiving for dress out. I grabbed my linens and state blues, along with cherished items I was taking home. When I got to receiving they made sure I was who I said I was. I signed paperwork for my discharge and received instructions to report to my probation officer within forty-eight hours. I was given a blue sweat suit and then escorted down the hall toward the gate.

Behold Your Mother

It had been nearly one year since I had heard from her. After countless letters returned followed by an ocean of tears and worry; she finally wrote me back. September 29, 2011, I would see my name on the mail list. An overwhelming sense of anxiety came over me. I showed the CO my inmate ID and then held the envelope in my hands. I went to my bunk, opened it and began reading the letter:

Dear Johnny,

I read your letter I'm not surprised, I know this sounds cold, but my son John has been gone for a long, long time. It is as if some evil entity took over and robbed him of his soul. You're not my son and haven't been for a long time. You are disrespectful, you constantly lie, manipulate and hurt. That evil mind of yours constantly plotting and planning. You use people, you enjoy hurting people, you embarrass me and I can't stand it. The only time there is a little peace in my life is when you are locked up, because then I know you are not able to use street drugs. I try not to even think about you, because I don't really have any good memories you. Except when you were little, before drugs. Don't even think about seeing your daughter. She's a happy and smart little girl and doesn't need your bad influence. You will never change!

Don't write me with your lies and promises, you are a con; you have had many years to change your life but you don't. I've lost all hope and finally accepted the fact that your mental illness is something I can't handle. You should have had some self-respect instead of arrogance. You could have been a loving, caring, and protective father—nope! You blew money on dope and whores instead. That child had needs and you were too selfish, that money was your late sister's blood money. Your mom (me) was struggling and busting her ass to pay bills and have a decent home. You could have helped me out with a portion of the bills. You acted like a mooch and wanted to live off of me for free. I owe you nothing! You disrespectful, ungrateful monster! This is one reason I refused to write you or read your letters. I get furious! I don't work at —— anymore. You had a hand in that, the stress was too much and —— wasn't very understanding about a lot of things. I was affected by all this stuff and having temporary custody of Layla. I was overwhelmed. I don't make the kind of money I made and I'm probably going to lose my house and everything I've worked for.

I have some bad news for you. Maybe you've already heard? Greg is dead. Heroin overdose. His little girl found him dead, poor kid she may be scarred for life. I guess it happened around two months ago. I just found out about a week ago. Damn! When you dumb asses wanna ride that train, that powerful locomotive will crush you! There is no hero in heroin he could have been a *hero* for his daughter. He could have loved her, supported her, and watched her grow up. He shattered her instead! She may or may not be able to pick up the pieces and be whole again. Then his poor mom, this may do her in.

Johnny, think about it.

Don't waste any time or money writing me, this is the last letter, I'm writing you. I may not be living here by the time you get out. Continue to take care of yourself, because nobody else can.

Mom.

It took a while for any type of emotions to register, after reading the letter I felt quite numb. I almost expected that type of response from her. It was all I could do, to pray; I prayed that God would continue to reveal what I needed to understand from my mother's words. I also prayed that he would teach me how to balance my emotions in moments of hurt, fear and anger. Everything my mother wrote about in that letter, was the mess that I left with her before going to prison. I couldn't be angry, I was a monster and yes an evil entity did take over. I had forgotten parts of just how ugly I had become to hurt my mother the way I did.

My soul started crying out in pain, I had to find a secluded place to grieve. Because I was in prison, it was forbidden to show moments of weakness. I then called my best friend in Virginia, she did like she always had done: listen and offer me some comforting words. It was good to know in the physical sense I wasn't completely alone. I think the pain was something I had to bear. I once read in some recovery literature, that pain was a great motivator for change; I found this to be completely true. Pain can either cripple you or you channel strength from the Lord and carry your own cross. I began to think of Jesus carrying the cross out of the praetorian toward Golgotha.

Even after being beaten, scourged and mocked; he still continued to press on. I thought about his mother Mary, how she must have felt as she watched her beloved son endure all his pain. When they raised him up on Calvary, Jesus's most beloved disciple John held Mary in his arms. From the cross Jesus cried, "Behold thy Mother." He then again cried, "Woman, behold thy son." To think I have allowed my mother to watch me torture myself for years, and no one was there to comfort her, was a soul reckoning experience.

I knew a change had occurred that was irreversible while in prison, it was deliverance. Everything in my life as bad as it was, had to occur to understand a purpose. Most people would not understand that, but I was given beauty from ashes. Jesus never asked for his punishment, he was not a criminal, but Jesus had to carry out his father's work and was then able to show grace to a wretch, like me. I felt such at peace, by God's affirmations. It was the peace that surpasses all understanding.

Later on that day, and into the evening I thought about my mother. Memories of good and bad, I yearned to tell her how much I loved her. She had been through hell and back, being abused and the death of her only daughter. A near-death of her son, and then my being sent into the devil's trophy case to leave her behind to clean up my mess. I knew that if I went back out and used heroin, my next stop would not be prison. I would die! I would die like my friends that passed away.

Inadvertently my mother was letting me know that if I died, it would kill her. She said it within the entire letter. I showed the letter to a couple of my Christian brothers, one in particular began crying and said, "How can you not be destroyed by this?" I had no explanation, other than Jesus. The old Johnny would've used that letter as an excuse to get drugs or drink booze. But not anymore! The Bible commands us to honor our mothers and fathers (Exodus 20:12) it is also written throughout the book of Proverbs, how a son is to conduct himself and honor his parents. Proverbs 19:26 says, "He that wasteth away his father and chaseth away his mother, is a son that causeth shame and bring reproach. I had chased away my mother, she tried with everything she knew how to do to be supportive, but it had caused her to become emotionally bankrupt.

I had pushed away my Mom, by my drug use and self-centeredness. I knew it was going to take action not words, and that I would need to respect her requests. I later would think about my friend who had overdosed. I thought about his mother, and my heart ached for her. She was much like a mother growing up to me, I spent many of nights at their house. During those years, we still had somewhat of an innocence. In her eyes, her son could absolutely do no wrong. As a matter of fact, when he and I would fight she would try to resolve our conflicts. I remember her always saying, "I know he's no angel but . . ." That was her famous line. Now her son was gone, he may have not been an angel, I just prayed the Angels took him home. As she looked over her son, as he lay dead in a casket; I prayed there was another Son there to comfort her. The Son of God . . .

The End Is Near

One October morning, after eating breakfast, while in the devil's trophy case, I was feeling very exhausted. I normally would make a strong cup of coffee, read my Bible and then go work out. But on this particular morning, I was too tired, I studied my Bible for a little bit and then fell asleep: I was in prison, yet it was another institution and it appeared to be a very rough one. The bunks were rusted, the walls were peeling paint, and there was an unfamiliar stench all throughout it. It still had the dorm atmosphere, and there were prisoners in their state blues littered everywhere, much like roaches if you flipped on a light switch. This place was huge and had me feeling very cautious. I bumped into a stocky young black guy while coming out of the bathroom.

He expressed some harsh words toward me, but I didn't refrain from my anger. I lashed back and told him if he wanted to continue having a problem, then we could solve it. I wasn't thinking about being a Christian, as a matter of fact it felt as though I was living in an old part of my life. Eventually he went his way, and I went mine. I went back out to the yard, and everywhere I looked, I saw men fighting like animals. It didn't matter what race or color were opposing one another, everyone was turning red. It was becoming a blood bath, and no one was doing anything to stop it. I went back inside of the dorm and saw the young black man I had words with. Seeing all the violence on the yard triggered something within me to apologize for what I had said to him. He didn't care to hear it though, in fact he gathered about a dozen of his buddies. As I sat at the table, they all surrounded me like a pack of vicious wolves.

Oddly enough I wasn't scared, I scanned for a way out and seized the opportunity to flee from them. I went outside again, relieved they didn't follow me. I approached this man in his late seventies or so; he was not an inmate, nor did he appear to be a staff member. In desperation I cried out to him, "Please you have got to get me out of here!" He was very calm while all the fighting continued around us, on the compound. I don't recall the exact words he said to me, but he took me with him into a building within the prison, so he could speak with a female staff member. I don't know what their conversation was about, but after they were done talking the senior citizen looked at me, smiled and said, "C'mon!"

Suddenly I found myself in a vehicle with the old man and another old man who was driving. They appeared to be happy and peaceful, but as for me I was still very distraught about all the violence I had witnessed and was concerned as to where they were taking me. I began talking to them about what I had experienced, as we traveled down the highway at an unusually fast speed. During the conversation, the older man who rescued me from prison said, "There's a reason you saw what you did, and I had to get you out of there, Johnny, because the end is near." I thought to myself, okay? I then said, "Where are we going?"

He replied by saying, "There is a woman who is interested in you. She's interested in helping you. She has a lot of questions about your drug abuse."

I said, "Okay? But what about my prison sentence?"

He told me, "I worked something out, we just ask that you cooperate so we can help each other."

I replied, "No problem!" We soon arrived at a futuristic looking building then got out of the vehicle. We entered the building and then boarded an elevator. Whether it was going up or down, I don't know? It was a long ride of nearly five minutes.

Eventually the doors opened and we walked down the hallway into a huge room. The room appeared to be a control center, with thousands of TV monitors mounted on a huge wall. I stared at the screens witnessing people caught in the grips of active addiction. People were getting high either smoking crack, shooting dope, or drinking alcohol. Some were weeping and cutting themselves. Every self-destructive possibility appeared on the wall of monitors. My heart was broken, I felt their pain. I began to cry, then turned my stare from the monitors and saw a petite middle aged woman. She said, "Hello, Johnny" with a smile.

I said, "Where am I?"

She then said, "Don't worry you are safe, and you are here to help me."

I woke up feeling very bewildered. I thought about this experience all day, and what significance it had toward my life. Science says that dreams are basically an account of our subconscious mind: fears, memories, and fantasies as we would like to see them. I didn't choose to look at things, from the scientific aspect. I don't follow science, faith and science contradict one another. Faith is the act of believing without seeing, while science is strictly based on evidence. My opinion of science, is man trying to play the role of God. I prayed for an understanding of this dream, was it really a look into the end? Or was it a demonstration on the purpose I would serve? I knew that upon my release, I would be doing something in the field of recovery full time.

I couldn't help but think about what I saw on those monitors, their souls crying out. I was familiar with that pain, all too well. I believed that old man who carried me out of prison was an Angel of the Lord. I believed the petite middle-aged woman worked closely with God. I also believed that in pursuit of helping addicts into recovery, she and I made a spiritual pact, to help one another. I had only seven months in prison to go, the end was drawing near.

87 Sundays

After returning from Nashville Tennessee, I was staying at my mother's house. My life had become completely destroyed, by nearly twenty years of drug addiction. I had ran with the devil for nearly thirty-one years, and there was nowhere to run anymore. The drugs and alcohol could no longer numb the pain. Inside, I felt as though a spiritual holocaust had taken place. I wanted to run from God, the devil had convinced me that I wasn't worthy of God's love. I was able to spend some time with Layla, but I couldn't feel for her.

I tried practicing the affirmation, that God would work everything out. I was being forced to surrender myself to the authorities, there was no way around it. When God is calling you, and you choose not to take heed to his voice and run; you will go nowhere. I still wanted to fight against it, and have things my way.

On Friday, August 6 of 2010, I was able to get some much-needed rest. I fell into a deep sleep, and found myself in a very large building much like a convention center. It wasn't anything out of the ordinary in its appearance, however there were stairwells and escalators all throughout the large room. It was filled with hundreds upon thousands of people. More and more were coming in as others were going out. I found myself standing in a line on the second floor within the building. I didn't engage in any conversations, and I don't quite remember what the other people around me were talking about. I veered over the balcony toward the ground floor, I saw tables set up and in front of them were lines of people moving toward them. Sitting behind the tables were men and women, dressed in robes and suits. Some were wearing black robes while others wore white. Those who were dressed in suits seemed as if they were security officers.

As I started down the stairwell, I thought to myself, "What is going on here?" I was boggled by how many people filled the room, and where could they have come from? Lines of people were everywhere, at the tables those dressed in robes sat in sequence, a white robe next to a black robe. The people consisted of various cultures, and race. After stepping onto the ground floor from the stairwell, I approached the table. I saw what appeared to be tickets, being handed over by those dressed in robes. The tickets were about 3½ inches in width, and about nine inches in length. I moved through the line and watched as the person in front of me was handed a ticket. I glanced at it briefly before I was handed mine. It was a transparent, grayish piece of plastic; as soon as it touched my hand, it became illuminated. It read my name, my birthdate and all types of information about me. It had a hologram effect, and was almost futuristic looking. There was cryptic writing on it that I could not interpret, but in large bold letters the ticket read DESTINATION HELL. I was being pushed through the line, I stopped angrily and turned toward one of the robed individuals. I wasn't sure what color robe they were wearing, but I asked them, "How did this happen!" He didn't give me an answer, he just stared right through me. I said I wanted some answers and that if I was going to hell, what happened to the apocalypse?

He replied, "In 87 Sundays."

The line of people were forcing me forward. I yelled back and then asked, "Where is my sister?"

Emotionless, he replied, "She is doing the work of God in before." Suddenly I was swallowed up in a huge crowd making its way toward the exit. I awakened completely distraught. I drank a cup of coffee and tried to collect my thoughts. I was puzzled by the 87 Sundays, what did this mean? Sure, it was a dream, but I thought there was a deeper significance. And what did it mean that my sister was doing the work of God, in before? Eventually my mother would wake up, then come into the living room. She sat down and had her coffee, I began to explain to her what happened. She stared at me wide-eyed with a concerned look on her face. My Mom started getting ready for work, as she was getting ready to leave she said, "Johnny, don't over think it, it was only a dream."

I couldn't help but ponder on it all day long. After my mother returned home, she told me she had thought about my dream all day too. She said that she had asked some friends what date that would equal to and the result was the first week of April 2012. I got out a calendar, and the date was April 1, 2012. The following week I turned myself into the county jail, on a Friday the thirteenth of 2010. It was the beginning of my living hell, I would spend twenty-one days in County lockup. That time would be credited along with time I served on probation violations toward my two-year prison sentence.

My prison term would closely equal to eighty-seven weeks. In other words, it was the fulfillment of 87 Sundays. My recollection of this dream would continue to resonate during my walk with Christ. I was already experiencing the living hell of prison, but I didn't want to go to an eternal hell for not honoring God's will. Ultimately, 87 Sundays is what inspired me to write this book. I didn't want to remain a dismal failure; I knew that if I were to serve God, then I had to become of service to others. In some relative way we all must face our own sentence of eighty-seven Sundays. It can manifest itself in so many ways; for me, it was prison. For someone else, it could be a simple as the loss of a career, a loss of a relationship or maybe depression, anxiety and fear. Either way, that time of suffering will come to pass. Not having a relationship with Christ can only lead to eternal suffering.

No Going Back

After becoming baptized in the Holy Spirit, God really began to take hold of my life. I prayed fervently for the blessing of spiritual gifts and would regularly fast. I wouldn't eat any food, only drink water. I would do this for three days straight on several occasions. A lot of prisoners based their happiness on food, so I thought it was the ultimate sacrifice I could make while serving out my sentence. The temptation would become overwhelming at times, as I watched other prisoners make "breaks" from ramen noodles.

While fasting, on the third day my hunger pains had grown very intense. It was like everyone in the dorm was cooking on this particular day, the smells of nachos, pizzas and breaks would cause my mouth to water. I wanted to prove my obedience to God, so I went to my bunk then prayed. I had become very tired and would soon fall asleep very hungry, and here is what happened: I found myself leaving prison, and I was going home. Somehow I would end up in a convenience store, I was very hungry and only had three dollars in the left pocket of my pants. As I walked around the store I thought about what could I spend the three dollars on, to satisfy my hunger? I thought about getting a microwave burrito, soda, and a bag of chips.

As I walked up and down the aisles I came upon a bin of pre-made sandwiches. The bread was something I had never seen before, there were also loaves of other breads that appeared to be of different ethnicity. I pondered on the thoughts of what sandwich I should purchase? I didn't get a sandwich, instead I got one of the prepackaged loaves, then removed the cellophane. It smelled delicious like it had been freshly baked. I prayed a blessing over the bread, then broke it and began eating it inside of the store.

While doing so, I noticed the store clerk staring at me from behind the checkout counter. I thought this guy must think that I'm stealing? So I said to the older gray-haired gentleman, "Don't worry, I've got this covered!" While patting the left pocket of my pants. He just nodded and then went back to his business, behind the checkout counter. I continued to walk through the store, while snacking on the delicious bread. I didn't get anything else, because I was satisfied by the bread alone.

I began approaching the checkout counter to pay the store clerk, while thanking him for his patience. I looked over the counter and there was another store clerk, I hadn't noticed before. He had a big smile on his face, and was a younger dark-haired man, that sat with his back rested against the wall. He seemed very interesting to me, he was human in form, but appeared to be something more. He started quoting Bible scriptures and was quoting it very rapidly. Every verse pertained to my situation, it was as if he knew what I had been through, without my ever saying a word. I found myself discussing scriptures with him.

He then asked me, "So you believe in the death, burial, and resurrection of Jesus Christ?"

I said, "Of course I do!"

He smiled and then veered his head upward, as if he saw something above. He then looked back at me and said, "So now that you are filled with the Holy Spirit, you will have to live the rest of your life this way."

He said very sternly, "There's no going back!"

I felt the sheer intensity and power of those words, we finished our conversation and he said, "God bless you." I returned by saying, "God bless you too." I then left the store, having been filled by the bread and the words that were spoken. The next day I would continue in my fast, I felt that I needed to show much more appreciation and sacrifice for God. I thought about the dream I had the previous night, and what it meant in comparison to the Holy Scriptures. I truly believed, that store clerk was a messenger of God. I believed that when he had looked upward, he was actually looking into the spiritual realm of heaven. All the day long, I kept telling myself, there was no going back. There was no going back to my evil ways, and no longer would I run with the devil. I began to meditate on Matthew 12:31: Wherefore I say unto you all manner of sin and blasphemy shall be forgiven unto men, but the blasphemy against the Holy Spirit shall not be forgiven unto men. I knew that Christ had performed a miracle in my life, and that the old Johnny must continue to die out. I knew that in the free world, I would face so many temptations. I also knew that I had to seek the Kingdom of God first, and his righteousness. I wanted to live a plentiful and meaningful life. I knew that there was no going back.

Narrow Is the Gate

utterflies began to set in my stomach, the walk down the corridor door toward the gate felt like an eternity. Just to the left of the gate was a small room, where I once again would have to be processed out. I waited on the CO for nearly twenty minutes to count out my gate pay, and to double check that my mug shot did indeed match me. The CO made a sarcastic remark about the tattoo on my neck and how it had changed.

Prior to going into London, the tattoo was of my initials in Japanese. While in prison, I had it covered up with a large cross, and the passage of Luke 9:23. I laughed off the CO's remarks and was then taken to the gate. I said a quick prayer asking for the Lord's protection before I entered into the free world. The guard from the control center would pop the lock on the gate, I entered inside where there was another gate to get through.

The first gate shut behind me, and the second gate popped open and I was officially released from the devil's trophy case. I made a slight turn into the waiting room, and was greeted by my best friend and her son. I gave them both big hugs and immediately said, "Let's get out of here!" We made our way toward the parking lot and then to her son's car. I was told to never look back at the prison when you are leaving, they said it was bad karma. I didn't follow the beliefs of karma, but did believe that you reap what you sow. I still didn't look back, we made our way down the road away from the prison compound, and toward the highway. The world had felt completely different since I had seen it last. It was almost like time had been suspended in some other dimension while I was doing my time in prison. My best friend asked if I was hungry. I was too anxious to eat. She then suggested that we go get some clothes and things I would need before I went back to her son's house. We went to a Walmart where I was able to get a couple of outfits, underwear, socks, blanket, pillow, and hygiene items. While walking around Walmart it felt as though I had come from another planet and discovered a new form of life. It was very awkward, but I refused to let it show. I got something to eat at a sandwich shop within the department store and to me it tasted as if it came from a five-star restaurant. I had spent nearly two years eating Ramen noodles and processed foods while in prison. I could have eaten a piece of shoe leather covered in gravy and it would've tasted better than prison food.

We made our way from the department store, got back into the car, and drove thirty or forty minutes back to Dayton. We arrived at my best friend's son's home and I was welcomed as if I were royalty. I was extremely grateful for the blessing of this family in my life. I got settled in, took a shower and knew the very next thing I must do was go to a recovery meeting. That evening I went to a meeting at my old home group. I walked up to people I once knew and reintroduced myself. I was welcomed with arms wide open. I was even able to reconnect with my former sponsor who I had lost touch with since my first prison number.

During the meeting I felt compelled to speak about my gratitude and knowing the importance of staying rooted in recovery. I never wanted to go back to prison and I never wanted to get high again. I got a list of names and numbers, and started building my peer support group. The very next day I would catch a bus to go meet with my probation officer. Being how close my penitentiary numbers were to each other I was placed on intensive probation.

My probation officer informed me that I must meet with them once a week until they thought I was fulfilling the terms of my probation. I was also informed that I was to stay away from my daughter's mother, and that if I followed the rules I could be off probation in one year. I went to as many meetings as I possibly could, I hung out with others in recovery afterward and began forming meaningful relationships.

On a Friday night I would catch a ride with a friend to a meeting just a little south of town. After getting out of the car and standing in the parking lot I saw someone who looked familiar to me. As I began approaching the building where the meeting was held, I noticed that it was Layla's mom. I looked over to my friend, and I said, "Man I don't think I should be here."

He looked at me kind of crazy and said, "Dude what's wrong?"

I informed him that a restraining order was in place, and that my daughter's mom was there.

He said, "Dude we should probably find another meeting." And we should have, but I had to know about my daughter. I approached Layla's mom and simply said, "If you have a problem with me being here, I will leave right now."

She said, "No, Johnny, this is where you need to be."

We made some small conversation, and I asked her how Layla was doing. She said that she was doing great and that she had thought about how she was going to tell her about me. Layla hadn't known that I was her Dad. Layla's mother had gotten married and the man she married was the only Dad Layla knew. From prison I had filed paperwork to establish my rights for visitation. Before leaving prison I received a court date and that date was in a couple weeks after being released. Layla's mom said that she wasn't going to deny me having a relationship with her, as long as I was doing what's right.

One afternoon after completing some errands, I took a bus to the neighborhood where my mother lived. I was very hesitant about knocking on her door because of the letter she sent me in prison. Actions will always speak louder than words, and I hadn't been home long at all to really establish anything. I still would go knock on the door and if by chance she wasn't home, I would just leave the CD I bought her inside of the screen door. I knocked and Mom answered the door, I smiled at her and said, "Hi Mom." She replied by saying, "It's my son, you're back." She told me she could see the life and light in my eyes, something she hadn't seen in a very long time. She welcomed me inside and we had a cup of coffee.

While making the coffee my mother told me that my biological father had died from a drug overdose while I was in prison. I thought about it for a second and then shed a few tears. My mother asked me why I was crying. I guess it was simply because I had hoped that one day he and I could establish a father/son relationship.

Mom changed the subject by telling me how smart and wonderful Layla was. I told her I ran into Layla's mom at a meeting and that I had a court date coming up to establish my visitation rights. She told me to be extremely careful, that she didn't trust Layla's mom one bit. I told her that I didn't plan on having any contact with her, other than to set up a time for me to reconnect with Layla. My mother agreed to take me when that day would occur.

We laughed, we cried and shared memories of past into present. Eventually I would say goodbye and tell my Mom how I was truly sorry, for all I had put her through. She encouraged me by saying she believed in me, and that I wanted to change. She said she loved me, and gave me a hug and I left to catch a bus and go back home. Layla's mom and I would make arrangements to meet at a park a few days later. She wanted Layla to feel comfortable around me before we established visitation. I went and bought Layla a little bicycle with training wheels on it. She was now just over three years old. My mother took me to the park, I got out of the vehicle and I could see her in the shelter house about thirty yards away.

Tears began to swell up in my eyes. I so desperately yearned for that day to see my little girl. Layla recognized my Mom because they were able to spend time together. My mom would say, "Layla look it's your Daddy!" But little Layla had a puzzled look on her face. She was actually scared of me, and that hurt, but I had been gone for so long. Slowly she began to warm up to me, and we played on the playground at the park. The time would come where we would have to leave. I couldn't even get a hug from little Layla, but I knew I had to be patient. I continued to keep myself busy by working out and making it to as many meetings as possible.

Within a week's time, I was asked to hold a service position at my home group meeting. I was entrusted with the key to the building and my responsibilities were to set up chairs, make coffee, place out the literature for newcomers, and then to facilitate the meeting. It was the first time in my life that I ever would maintain a position of responsibility. Opening that meeting allowed me to get out of myself and my self-centered nature. I knew that there were people who depended on me to be there. Maybe these same people would come through those doors the same way I was three years ago, in desperation of hope. The following week I would go to court and establish my visitation rights. Everything seemed to be falling into place. I went to church with my best friend's son on a couple of occasions. He belonged to a Pentecostal church that was less than a quarter of a mile away from where we were living.

It wasn't that the church was bad, but I just didn't feel welcomed. I could have been just over thinking what others thought of me? "The scary-looking tattooed guy?" I expressed wanting to check out some other churches to my best friend's son. He told me there was a biker Church that I probably would really enjoy. Sounded like a great place for me! Tattoos, leather, rock 'n' roll, Harley-Davidson's, but more importantly Jesus! So I decided that one Sunday I would go and check it out.

It wouldn't take long and Layla's mother would tell me that she and her husband were getting a divorce, then start making flirtatious passes at me. There was a small part within me that thought, "She's in recovery now. Maybe things could be different?"

Being in recovery doesn't always equal sanity and serenity for others. It didn't take long for me to realize the toxic nature in my dealings with her. I told her that if she didn't drop the restraining order, I had nothing more to say to her. Eventually she did, but I still had to follow the rules of my probation. I told my probation officer there was no longer a restraining order in place, and that I needed to maintain minimal contact for the sake of visiting with my child. I also explained the toxic nature of Layla's mom, and that my probation officer would need to trust me and I would do nothing to break the law. I understood the importance of needing to create stability and a future for myself and my daughter.

Daily, I diligently worked toward bettering myself. I enrolled in the local community college for dietetics and nutrition management. I was still very passionate about working out, my mother purchased me a membership at a local recreation center and I would often make the two-mile run to the facility, to work out. Working out allowed me to cope with stress, anxiety and was the antidote against depression. I would take out a student loan and move-in to my first apartment. I started school and still made it to recovery meetings as much as possible. I also began attending the biker Church my friend suggested I go to.

I felt like I was actually getting somewhere in my life and moving at a rapid pace. I was spending quality time with my daughter and our bond was strengthening with every visit. While at my mother's one afternoon she expressed concern because Layla kept itching at her head. My mother suggested that we look through her hair to see if she had head lice. Sure enough she did, bugs and eggs were infested throughout her hair. I immediately went to a drugstore to purchase a lice removal kit, Layla didn't like the experience very much. We then went back to my apartment and I stripped all the linens, pillow cases and her clothing to put into the wash.

I contacted Layla's mother and asked her if she was aware that Layla had lice? She said no, but I believed this to be a lie because this type of infestation couldn't have happened in just two days. My mother and I took Layla home. The weekend that Layla would return, I checked her head again and sure enough she still had lice. I became angry and irritated, I didn't want Layla to feel like she had done something wrong. After all, it wasn't her fault. I sensed there was neglect concerning Layla while at her mom's house. I asked Layla a series of questions such as do you brush your teeth at night, do you take a bath regularly, do you always have clean clothes, is your room clean? Some of these questions she could not answer, she was only three years old. Every time that I would get Layla she would always have lice. Her mother blamed it on the kids that Layla played with. She would never assume responsibility for taking care of it.

I spent over $200 in lice removal products, my mother even bought an electric comb that would kill the bugs and nits by an electric shock. One afternoon I would receive a phone call from Layla's grandmother on her mother's side of the family. She said that it was important that I get my daughter out of her mother's home. She also said that Layla has had lice for over two years, she then told me she had witnessed firsthand neglect and physical abuse by her mother toward Layla. I immediately went downtown to the courts building.

I filed for a temporary protection order on Layla's mother toward Layla. I went before a magistrate and at first she didn't want to hear what I had to say. I expressed my sincere concerns for the safety and welfare of my daughter. Something I said must have resonated, because she granted the temporary protection order and told me the Montgomery County Sheriff's would be contacting me to come pick up my daughter. Later on that night I was contacted by the Sheriff and I went and picked up Layla. Layla was upset she didn't want to be taken from her mom, I didn't want to take her from her either. I just needed to make sure that she was taken care of. Having Layla with me allowed me to feel at peace and taught me so much about being a parent. At the same time it made it hard to focus on my school studies.

Finals were coming up; the semester would be coming to a close. I couldn't always rely on my mother to babysit Layla so I missed many days of school and failed two classes at the end of the semester. I dropped out of school to focus on being a parent and trying to make more money. I was cooking burgers at a small restaurant down the street from my apartment. Some days I would have to take Layla with me and she would have to sit in a booth for a few hours with her toys and coloring books, until my mom could pick her up.

It wasn't easy being a parent without a driver's license, a vehicle or a babysitter I could depend on. At least I had a safe and clean home where all of Layla's needs were met. We were able to do a lot of fun things we would go to the library, we would rent movies, order pizza and go to the park right behind my apartment. Layla thought the park belonged to me because it was literally right outside my back door.

After about a month of Layla staying with me, I had to go back to court in regards of the TPO for Layla. Layla's mother had gotten an attorney but I could not afford one. My past which wasn't too far from me was maliciously used to make me look like a horrible person. Layla was ordered back to her mother, and later on that evening I had to take her back. As a result of me taking Layla from her Mom's home, Layla's mother thought it would be appropriate to punish me by keeping Layla from me. She did this for a little over a month. Fortunately I was able to draw strength from church and meetings of recovery. It wasn't easy, whenever I would feel hurt I would turn it into anger, and usually that anger would lead to violence.

I had to do a lot of praying and trust that God had a plan and would make sure my daughter was okay. Around this same time, I would run into an old acquaintance who played drums for another band while I was in Edge of Life. It had been nearly ten years since I had seen him. He said that he had wondered what happened to me after those painful years in 2004 and 2005.

We sat, talked and reminisced on those days. He professed that he had devoted his life to serving Christ, and that he was trying to start a band. At the time I wasn't really looking for a band, but I was intrigued to listen to his ideas. He said that he already had some ideas for songs, not only was he a drummer but he could also play guitar. We exchanged numbers and several days later we met up and began writing music together.

In a short period of time, we were able to come up with enough material, to start performing at some acoustic coffee shop gigs. He didn't work full time and neither did I so we worked diligently on writing original songs. I invited him to come to the biker church with me on one Sunday, and he fell in love with it. I was now able to make it to church more regularly because he would come pick me up on Sunday mornings. Music had always allowed me to channel my emotions into a song. It helped with coping on all the stress that surrounded living life on its own terms.

Eventually Layla's mom would allow me to start seeing her again. But once again she would have lice, come over in clothes too small or soiled, and unbathed. It was all I could do, to bite my tongue. I had to, or at least I thought I had to because I was in fear of Layla being taken away from me again. All I wanted to do was spend time with my daughter, live sober, make music and serve Jesus Christ. I often thought about my days in prison up to my day coming home. I had extreme gratitude for all the blessings I had received in such a short amount of time. I was living up to God's Word, to the best of my abilities.

Risen from the Fall

In 2004, after my sister had passed away, I began questioning the afterlife. I didn't have a relationship with Christ, so I questioned many different philosophies based on world religions. I wanted to know where my little sister was, and that she was safe. Shortly after her passing, one night I was in a department store at about 2:00 a.m. I was very depressed and grieving the loss of her. I was looking at CD's in the music section of the store, I noticed some artwork on a CD cover that really stood out to me. On the cover was a man with his arms spread out as if he had broken chains. The CD belonged to a band named Pillar.

Right next to that very CD was another CD by Pillar, and it was entitled *Where Do We Go from Here*. The artwork showed a bird ascending, and had a beautiful picture of a landscape that looked as if it were taken in the Mojave Desert region. I picked up the CD and began reading the song titles on the back. I had never heard of the band, but something about that CD caused me to purchase it. That album would get me through some very dark days, and little did I know they were a Christian band. Nor did I know just how much that band would have an impact on my life nine years later. One afternoon during the summer of 2013 my drummer introduced me to a guitar riff that he had been working on. It spoke to my soul, I immediately recalled that painful day in prison where I turned my life over to Christ and was delivered from my addiction.

Words effortlessly poured onto the notebook as I began writing what would later be called "Hard to Swallow." Later on that day we would record the song in my drummer's home studio. A few days later my drummer would call me and say that he was coming over with some amazing news. I wasn't sure what to expect, but when he arrived at my apartment he was ecstatic with joy. Apparently he had shared our song on a Facebook page that belonged to Noah Henson. Noah Henson was the guitar player of the band Pillar.

My drummer proceeded to tell me that Noah was thoroughly impressed by the song and said we needed to make an album. I didn't know what to think, it all seemed very surreal to me. My drummer made arrangements for us to speak with Noah who had become a producer and was passionate about artist development. A day or so later we spoke with Noah over the telephone, he informed us that he was interested in recording and producing us in his home studio located in Nashville Tennessee. I couldn't believe it, Noah was one of my guitar heroes and I felt it would be an accomplished dream to write a record with him. We discussed finances and travel and then set a date to venture to Nashville.

One Sunday morning while at biker church, just when I thought my life couldn't get much better I heard the voice of an angel. She was leading worship and had the most beautiful voice I had ever heard. I could feel the Holy Spirit moving at 1,000 mph, and I could feel the anointing and passion as she sang. I did not know who she was but after that service all I could think was *Wow!* My drummer would later tell me that her name was (for the sake of protecting her anonymity) Melody, his wife would also say she thought she was single and the two of us would make a great couple. I just laughed it off, and pretended as if I wasn't that interested.

Later on that day, I would look her up on Facebook. I couldn't help but adore her beauty in the photos she had posted. About a week or so later my drummer informed me that the biker church we belonged to was excited to hear about our upcoming studio venture to Nashville. He also told me that Melody had contacted him and asked if we were interested in leading worship with her on a Sunday to help raise money for our trip.

I said, "Sure, let's do it!"

My drummer wouldn't be available, but he suggested that I contact Melody and discuss the details. So I did just that, we messaged back and forth through Facebook and discussed what songs we would play for the following Sunday's worship set. When Sunday arrived I had arranged for someone who belonged to the motorcycle ministry to pick me up. I still didn't have a license so relying on rides to get where I needed to be was very difficult. My ride stood me up, I started to panic because I thought I was going to blow the opportunity of singing with this gorgeous woman. I contacted Melody and told her I was stuck at home.

She said not to worry and that she could be at my place in twenty minutes. That would only leave us ten minutes before service would start, and I never officially had a rehearsal with her or the worship team. She picked me up and I could tell she was extremely nervous. Not because of me, but simply because of the strict time frame we were trying to work in. We made it to biker church with five minutes to spare and was able to rehearse through one song. In moments like that all you can do is pray and give it to God, so that's exactly what we did. The worship set went over very well with the congregation, after church many people would say that we should sing together more. And we would do just that.

By the contributions from those at biker church and by playing small acoustic coffee-shop shows, my drummer and I were able to raise a significant amount of money toward our recording trip. The day had finally arrived, we loaded our things into my drummer's SUV, stopped and filled up the gas tank and hit the road. The trip was only about a five-hour drive. We jammed out to Pillar CD's and talked about how we thought Noah's house would look, or what kind of car he would drive. When we got into Nashville, we called Noah and he suggested that we meet at a Mexican restaurant to discuss our plans. We pulled into the restaurant parking lot, and expected to see him pull up in a brand-new Mercedes or BMW. We waited for about five minutes and Noah pulled up in a Mazda Tribute SUV. He got out of the car and threw back his long dreadlocks that were down to the backs of his knees.

He approached us and said, "What's up fellas, let's do this!" We all went inside, sat down and introduced ourselves. Noah was extremely laid-back and easy to talk to. We ate and discussed our approach to recording our first song, we would only be in town for three days so we needed to work diligently. After conversation and having dinner, we followed Noah back to his house. His home wasn't anything extraordinary but it was still rather nice. We went inside and met his wife and kids, they were very warm and welcoming toward us. He then showed us the studio, and some material that he had produced in the past.

The sound quality was amazing, it was hard to believe that he could produce such amazing work in his little home studio. We didn't waste any time toward getting into writing a song, I compiled several pages of lyrical ideas but had no clue about what my vocal melody approach would be. After laying the foundation with all the instruments of the song, it was my turn to record. I was extremely nervous being that my creative abilities were exposed before one of my guitar heroes. Noah was very encouraging and told me to relax. I started getting into the groove and we worked on the song until the wee hours of the morning.

We were all exhausted, so it was time for some rest. As I lay there in that studio on his futon, I couldn't help but think about how powerful God truly was, and how my being at Noah Henson's house nine years after my sister passed, was a divine appointment. I couldn't help but think about my little sister and what it must have been like before she entered the gates of heaven. Revelation 21:4 says, "He will wipe away every tear from their eyes, and death shall be no more, neither shall there be mourning, nor crying, nor pain anymore, for the former things have passed away."

I found comfort and rest in thinking that my little sister stood before Jesus and plead with him to help me stay sober and to bless my musical endeavors before he wiped away those last tears. For the first time in my life, I felt as though I was making music for the right reasons and that God was going to make his move in a very powerful way. We worked on the song for the next couple days until we completed it and would have to head back to Ohio.

Working with Noah was such a learning experience and we had created a bond that was inseparable. When we returned home very excited to share our song with our family at biker church. Everyone loved the new song, we had the full support of almost everyone that made up the congregation. I had never felt so content in my life. I started spending more time with Melody, and my feelings grew stronger for her every day. Melody had just come out of a relationship where she was engaged to be married. She called the wedding off for reasons that I didn't know, but told me that her ex-fiancé wasn't supportive of her musical ambitions. It was rather selfish of me to want to establish a relationship with her after she had just come out of a relationship. We were spending time together like a committed couple, but without verbalizing the commitment.

I didn't handle that too well. I wanted things my way. On more than one occasion I would shut her out and back away. I did this because I didn't want to get my heart broken. I focused on the music that my drummer and I were working on and we continued to make trips back and forth to Nashville to record with Noah. There was something about Melody that I couldn't completely let go of. And I don't know what it was about me but it must've been the same for her. We would still spend time together and do things that a committed couple would do, but still never verbalized the commitment. Everyone in the church saw us as a couple, the pastor even began asking questions about our dealings with one another. I didn't like his approach due to the fact he addressed his questions toward my drummer and not me. I started forming a resentment toward the pastor of the biker church. I continued to go to church there simply because I loved the people that were part of the church. So to release some steam off of the pressure cooker, I focused on my recovery and outreach ventures. I began establishing myself as a well-respected person in recovery by my community. When I had started using heroin, it was a drug that wasn't so readily available as it was when I came home from prison. Heroin had become an epidemic that plagued the city of Dayton. The city I lived in was number two in heroin the nation for overdose related deaths. I would meet with various recovery groups, neighborhood drug coalitions, and share my experiences with treatment centers. Being of service to my community, other addicts, and their families; ultimately, it is what kept me clean. I used my music as a platform to promote the benefits of recovery as well as the unconditional love of Jesus Christ. It started becoming my experience that whenever I was working toward furthering the kingdom of heaven, I would experience severe spiritual attacks.

In Ephesians 6, it speaks about putting on the whole armor of God and protecting us from the fiery darts of the enemy, but those darts began to feel like cannonballs. I began to feel very oppressed. I also started having a lot of arguments with not only my drummer, but with Melody. I had felt that my drummer's ego was becoming very inflated and that I would never get the commitment I yearn for, or acceptance from Melody that I desired. I had been dating her for nearly a year and still hadn't met her family. I also began to suspect that she was still in contact with her ex-fiancé. The dramatic nature of my dealings with my drummer and Melody and the resentments toward my pastor at the church started pushing me into isolation.

I started becoming very bitter, but because who I was in the eyes of the recovery community and my church I put on the false appearance, that everything was okay. Melody began to change about her affection toward me. She went above and beyond trying to comfort me. On Christmas of 2014, she had secretly contacted my friends and people of the church to help with getting my driver's license back. It was an amazing Christmas. I felt extremely loved and blessed. My church family was so giving to also make sure Layla had an amazing Christmas.

My band continued to play shows and make trips back and forth to Noah's in Nashville to record. Although Noah, my drummer, and myself would do all the writing; we hadn't become a full band. We enlisted in a battle of the bands competition, over the course of three months we were able to move into the final rounds of the competition.

We took second place. I was grateful that we had made it that far, but things didn't settle well with my drummer. It seemed as though he felt a sense of entitlement, his attitude disgusted me and I thought it was necessary to hold him accountable. That conversation would escalate into my leaving the band. Eventually he humbled himself and we were able to finish the last two songs toward our album. I was still going to biker church around this time but I no longer felt spiritually connected to it. I became aware of all the politics and self-righteousness by people that professed themselves to be leaders. One day I scheduled to meet with the pastor to discuss my feelings toward him and the church. He basically told me that if I didn't agree with the way things were handled, that I should find another church. I couldn't believe that someone who was supposed to be a shepherd for Jesus, would cast them out of the flock. So I stopped going to biker church for a while. I also felt it necessary to put space between my drummer and I, as well as Melody. I had a friend that I've known for 20+ years from my old neighborhood. Instead of being the drug user, he lived the lifestyle of being the drug dealer. Through a series of unfortunate circumstances he made it out of the dope game and began living for Jesus.

He admired all the work that I did within recovery communities, and wanted to be a part of the movement. He suggested that we form a Rap/Rock group with a Christ centered message. At first I declined, I wasn't a rapper and I didn't care much for rap music. He was very persistent, and one day I finally agreed to do some writing. We called ourselves Kill the Epidemic, and the first song we would write was toward the antiheroin movement called Take the City Back. It received a lot of attention, it also opened doors in the recovery community for us to share our stories and our music. I was now a little over three years clean, I continued to be a part of my other band but things just weren't the same. I also would continue to spend time with Melody but my feelings became very bitter toward her. It was too easy to shut her out and cut off communication with her. She never gave up on me and pled for me to change how I acted toward her. My pride and arrogance would nearly ruin my relationship with her.

In the summer of 2014, my band was finally ready to release the album we had recorded in Nashville. Prior to our release show, I sensed dishonesty from my drummer when it pertained to the finances of our band. He lied about how much the overhead cost was for sound and production. I figured if he would lie about something as petty as that, what else had he lied about? Needless to say, I bit my lip for the sake of our fans and played the show.

A few days after the show, I would confront my drummer about his dishonesty and his attitude of entitlement toward everything the band had equally worked for. The conversation escalated into an angst filled argument rather quickly. I decided not to throw any more gasoline on the fire and got off of the phone. A few hours later, I discovered on Facebook that I had been removed from the band. This infuriated me for many reasons. One, because I had written every lyric and vocal melody that pertained to our songs. Two, because of the unprofessional way my drummer went about things. Three he had lied horribly on more than one occasion. And finally because he was trying to take ownership of songs that pertained to my life's story.

This experience drove me deeper into a hole of bitterness, anger, isolation and verbal outbursts. Those who I proclaimed to care about the most would receive the blunt of my frustrations. Especially Melody, she tried to be as supportive as she could and I would only push her away. My neighborhood friend whom I had known for many years would convince me to focus on Kill the Epidemic so I could continue to utilize my creative abilities. Although people loved the music we made, I could never feel connected to it.

It just wasn't my thing, I prayed for God to open another door of opportunity with rock music. I felt as though my purpose and dreams were destroyed, so I prayed that God would allow me to pick up the pieces and together we would build something everlasting. One morning while lying in my bed, just as plain as day I heard the Holy Spirit say to me, "John, although that band is done, you will become Risen from the Fall." I had no idea what this meant, but I trusted that God would one day reveal it. Shortly after my departure from the band I was notified that my drummer had went to the pastor of biker church and disclosed things that I had only confided in him.

My drummer was trying to destroy my reputation. I had enough of the politics, the backbiting and poor examples of holiness at the biker church. I made the choice to leave that summer, and take a break from church altogether. Apparently I wasn't the only one who had enough of the misdeeds at biker church, Melody would soon leave and so would my neighborhood friend and his family. It wasn't long after that, most of the members that belonged to the motorcycle ministry would leave also. Not being involved with a church, did not help me to grow spiritually. I continued to read my Bible and watch sermons online, but lacked the Fellowship with like-minded believers to hold me accountable. I began backsliding, I began looking for outward things to fill the inward voids in my life.

In October of 2014, I broke things off with Melody. In my mind, I was completely done with her, but I hadn't resolved the feelings I had for her in my heart. I began entertaining the idea that I should date other women, and although Melody would not give up. I was always stubborn and cold hearted toward her. In late October or early November I contacted Noah with my ideas to start another band. I would use the name Risen from the Fall, which was given to me by the Holy Spirit. Noah sent me an idea that he had been working on, and I immediately began writing lyrics for it. I would also arrange for an acoustic fundraising event to help gather money in hopes of making it to Nashville to record. Melody would help me arrange this event, I hadn't completely severed ties with her.

I also did not care that I was stringing her along, I justified it by feeling like she had done that to me for the last year. I would make it back to Nashville, and record the very first song toward the Risen from the Fall EP. The song was called "On the Inside" and was about the passion you have about completing your goals, even though everyone around you is trying to tear you down. I returned back to Ohio even though I was blessed to be moving forward, I was still very bitter, angry and arrogant. I cut off all contact with Melody and began hanging out with another girl I had went to high school with. I didn't care how Melody felt about it, so she eventually started seeing her ex-fiancé again. I didn't care about the girl I was dating, she was only someone to compensate the loneliness I felt. After about a month I had a moment of clarity, I contacted my neighborhood friend and said that I was thinking a lot about Melody. He was relieved to know I had a change of heart, but at the same time he thought it was too late. I messaged Melody and told her how sorry I was for being so selfish, cold and mean. I think she was rather shocked that I reached out to her.

Just before Christmas, I had a show with Kill the Epidemic. Melody came to the show with some of her girlfriends from work. Something felt strange about the way she acted toward me. Later on that night after the show, I was home and scrolling through Facebook, I came across some pictures of Melody and her ex-fiancé, that were taken a couple days previously. I felt instant hurt that quickly turned into anger, I got into my car and drove to Melody's house and discovered a vehicle with Missouri license plates. The vehicle belonged to her ex-fiancé, who was in town to visit her for the holidays. The situation would cripple me emotionally, I truly thought that I had lost Melody for good. I knew that if I were going to get her back, I would have to make some huge changes. After Christmas Melody left with her ex-fiancé to visit with friends and family in Missouri. She didn't return until days after the New Year.

During that time she also lost an uncle from a drug overdose in Georgia. As soon as she returned to Ohio, she then left to Georgia for the funeral. I had never felt such intense emotions while being sober, until up to this point I hadn't had much trouble working through my feelings. I couldn't eat, I couldn't sleep or control my crying. I began to actually see and feel how special of a person Melody truly was. I had to hold myself accountable for my actions, you can only push a person away for so long before they finally choose to move on. Melody eventually returned back to Ohio, she was unsure about seeing me because of all that had taken place. Her family did not approve of me and at the time thought I was psychotic. In many ways I was, driving by her house and constantly texting her. The only relief that I found was to keep myself busy by writing songs and going to church.

By this time I started attending a church called Sons of Light Ministries. Sons of Light was made up of members who previously went to the same biker church I had left. They empathized with my brokenness and were there for me during my moments of fear and doubt. Suddenly one day I had an epiphany, I had written a song that was about the hurt and fear I was experiencing as a result of Melody and my breakup. Other than leading worship Melody and I had never really made music together. I had the idea of her singing with me on this new song called "Knot in Vein." Sons of Light allowed me to hold a fundraising event toward getting back to Nashville.

At first Melody declined with wanting to sing on the song, she felt there hadn't been enough time and space to think things through. I was able to raise enough money to get back to Nashville some time in February. Melody would be in Nashville at the same time for a work seminar. On the day I arrived in Nashville I explained to Noah what I was feeling in correlation with the song. He immediately went to work on creating the foundation for the song. Into the early hours of the morning we wrote and recorded, the song came almost effortlessly.

The next day Melody contacted me and said that she was willing to sing on the song and would be arriving at Noah's within the hour. I was extremely happy but nervous at the same time. When Melody arrived I had butterflies in my stomach much like the very same day I lead worship with her at biker church. She came into the studio and Noah began playing the song, I could see that she was definitely feeling the spirit of the music. I had already pretty much tracked all the vocal parts, so Noah asked Melody if she was ready to sing.

She responded yes and went into the vocal booth and laid the most amazing vocal tracks in only about an hour. She was a natural in the studio and brought a natural creative element to write beautiful vocal melodies. I knew right then and there, in that moment she needed to become a part of Risen from the Fall. She said that she would think about it. I was okay with that. I didn't want her to feel pressured. On the way back to Ohio, I did a lot of soul-searching. I began to analyze just how self-centered and inconsiderate I was even after being four years sober. I knew that it was time to get back to the basics. I also knew that it was time to let go completely of the resentment and fears that had nearly destroyed my relationship with Melody. She had been the only woman I ever dated that truly loved me and had my back in situations most people would run from. Especially when it pertained to Layla.

My dealings with Layla's mother had never gotten any better, Layla would still come over with lice, soiled clothes and tell us that her Mommy would sleep all day. I would soon discover that Layla's mother was getting high again. I started thinking about all that I would need to do, if I were to fight for custody and win? I also began thinking about my future with Melody and if we were ever to get married, I would need a bigger place.

I always had a yearning to have a family of my own, one that would sit down and pray at the dinner table together. A family that would take vacations, and a family whose home would be filled with love, laughter, and cherished memories. I was still living in a one-bedroom apartment, so I began looking to see if there were any houses for rent within my budget. I made a post on Facebook and was messaged by a woman who belonged to one of the recovery groups I was affiliated with. Her daughter was caught in the grips of her addiction, but this woman valued and saw something in me that gave her hope for her daughter one day getting sober.

She messaged me the address and said to take a look at the house and if I was interested, she would work out a rent payment within my budget. I drove over to the house and immediately fell in love with it. It was a small two-bedroom with a finished basement, and a huge yard, in a quiet little neighborhood. I met with her and her husband and told them I definitely was interested in renting the house. They drew up a lease agreement and I was able to move-in shortly after Valentine's Day. They also said that if I was interested in buying it, they would be willing to sell it to me on a land contract.

Because I made the choice to "let go and let God," my life became abundantly blessed, Melody and I were able to form a band around the songs we had written. We started playing a variety of shows and were able to use our music to minister people. My church family was even able to find a building to become a full-fledged church, and provide outreach for the drug infested neighborhoods of East Dayton. It astonished me how much of an impact heroin had made on the Dayton area When I first started using heroin, it was a drug that wasn't widely available, and if you did it, you might as well have been written off by society.

Now heroin was everywhere! Driving through my city streets almost resembled episodes of *The Walking Dead*. But I would continue to do my small part of sharing the blessings of my recovery with others, and testify to the power of Christ before churches, recovery rallies, treatment centers and one on one interventions.

One evening while at home I received a message that a water line had busted inside of the building Sons of Light Ministries had moved into. It was about 9:00 p.m., so I suggested to Melody we should go down to the building and help out our church family. Apparently we arrived a little too late, and they had temporarily resolved the issue and so we left. My daughter was living in a house about a block and a half away from the church. I drove by the house and discovered Layla playing outside while her older sister sat on the front porch with her face in her phone.

I pulled over on the curb, rolled the window down and said to Layla she needed to get inside and start getting ready for bed. I also told her that I would be there to pick her up that forthcoming weekend and we were going to have a great time. I told her I loved her, watched her go inside of the house and drove away. Not even five minutes after I returned home, Layla's mother started calling my phone. She called repeatedly, but I refused to answer because I knew that the conversation would be hostile. She then began texting me and I basically told her that I had enough of the neglect and poor excuses of why my child was living the way that she was. I told her that I would be fighting for custody, due to her mother's irresponsibilities.

The very next day I was helping a friend do some landscaping at his home. I noticed I had missed a call on my cell phone, but received a voice mail. I checked the voice mail, and discovered it was the Montgomery County Sheriff's office saying that I needed to contact them. I returned the phone call and spoke with the Sheriff who informed me that my child's mother had taken a temporary protection order out on me. Apparently, she made accusations that I threatened to kidnap Layla and that she and her family were in fear of their safety. It was hard to stay motivated and work the rest of the day. I did what I needed to do to help finish my friend with his land-scaping, then made my way home.

The next day, I went down to the courts building to receive my copy of the temporary protection order. Within the order Layla's mother's statement ensued that I was mentally unstable and off of my medications, that I had threatened her with violence and to kidnap my daughter. She also falsely accused me of shooting steroids. It was very discouraging to read these false accusations and have to defend my integrity. Luckily I had been preparing for a situation such as this and saved all the text messages between Layla's mother and myself. I also had pictures of the lice in her head and soiled clothes that she would wear when I would pick her up.

After my pastor at church discovered what was happening he contacted me and suggested that I get in touch with the attorney he worked for. I wasn't in a position to spend thousands of dollars on legal services, however my Pastor spoke with him and the attorney said he would represent me pro-bono at the protection order hearing. During my consultation with him he suggested that I fight for full custody of Layla, he also warned me that it would be not only expensive but a time-consuming process. On the day of the hearing for the protection order. Layla's mother was a no-show. Simply because she knew that she had lied and I had evidence to support that. Two weeks later the temporary protection order was dropped. I then met again with the attorney to discuss his approach toward a custody hearing. In order to hire him, he would need a $2,000 retainer fee. I didn't have that kind of money, nor did I know how I was going to get it. It was the fall season of 2015, and I was painting a house for Melody's brother-in-law.

I stepped outside to take a small break and my phone began to ring with a number I did not recognize. I answered the phone and some man asked to speak with me quoting my full name.

I said, "This is he." He began then telling me that he was an attorney representing the estate of my late grandmother on my biological father's side. He also informed me that his firm was trying to locate me for several years. They had found me from one of my YouTube music videos and then traced it to my artist page on Facebook. The attorney said that he had some paperwork that he needed to send me and that it needed to be signed and notarized so he could begin the payout process of my grandmother's estate.

I asked him, "Just about how much are we talking about here?"

He said, "Several thousands of dollars."

This most certainly was a situation ordained by God. I would've never expected to receive anything from that side of my family. Due to my biological father's overdose I was listed as next of kin along with my younger brother and Aunt who was the head beneficiary of my grandmothers will. After getting off the phone I excitedly called Melody to tell her the good news. It would take several months before receiving a payout; however, on Christmas Day I was with Melody and her family. I had never experienced a Christmas with such a loving family atmosphere. They made me feel welcomed and loved.

As we exchanged gifts, I was given an envelope and inside of it was a receipt for the retaining fee to my attorney that was paid for by Melody's dad. I felt a sense of peace that everything was going to be okay. Even in the midst of my missing Layla I was blessed beyond words. Those were some of the best days that I spent with Melody in renewing our relationship. I developed a bond with her family and tried to earnestly help her brother with his alcoholism and mental health issues. I was beyond helping him because he didn't possess the desire to change. That's the absurdity of addiction; it will make a holocaust of your life and lie to you, making you think that things couldn't be better. Her brother would experience multiple hospital-izations and inpatient treatment stays only to go back home to his parents' barn and drink himself into oblivion.

During the court proceedings the band stayed relatively busy. However it was hard to break beyond a local scene without finances or management. It also became very frustrating to try and book studio time with Noah because he was constantly on the road. Not only that, he had a newborn daughter and other studio clients that he was trying to catch up with on their work. I began to feel an intense strain and exhaustion from trying to control outcomes-based on my will. I had become saturated with the things concerning Layla, my relationship with Melody, and trying to keep the band working. Melody began feeling the strain too.

My insecurities, paranoia, and moods of frustration started pushing her away again. She encouraged me that I had to fight with everything to get custody of Layla. I thought her motive was simply because she didn't like Layla's mom. I just wanted to see my daughter. Months turned in to a year. I became depressed and I also had a falling out with my long time childhood friend who I had started Kill the Epidemic with. The only sense of relief I felt was by spending some money after receiving the payout from my grandmother's estate.

I bought a dependable car and that coming summer I bought a motorcycle. It was still my addictive nature to seek outward things to try and fill inward voids. Riding a motorcycle though allowed me to feel a sense of freedom that I had never felt in my entire life. It became my new drug. Sadly, one of the first times I was able to ride it was during the last ride of a close friend from church who had passed away from cancer. That was the beginning of grief and the deaths of loved ones that I would soon encounter.

I had become complacent with my church attendance, recovery meeting attendance, and step work. The result was pain, irritability, depression and isolation. I was becoming burnt out on music; it had even caused Melody and I to start butting heads. I had a vision that I thought was God inspired and with each new member I compromised that vision until it became something that I didn't want. We enlisted a guitar player who had a lot of "universalist" views that compromised my boldness and what I thought should be said lyrically. I began thinking Melody was talking to or seeing someone else; this only broadened the gap between us and made communicating virtually impossible. Not only that, we never fully resolved our past issues with one another. It was like putting a Band-Aid on a broken leg. We continued to go through the motions of seeing one another, but her heart had journeyed elsewhere.

One afternoon I rode my bike out to Melody's house. When I pulled into the driveway, I shut the bike off and felt my phone vibrating in my pocket. I had received a text message from my mother saying to call her as soon as possible, that my Aunt had committed suicide. I frantically called, and she informed me that my Aunt was gone. Not only was I in shock but also in disbelief! My Aunt was a strong woman who had been through abusive relationships, and left with nothing but the clothes on her back and her children, she made a way for them to live in a better area and to go to better schools.

Childhood memories came flooding from my heart and poured into my mind playing film clips almost as if it were an old-fashioned reel to reel projector. My aunt was very well aware of the abuse I experienced growing up and she would take my cousins, my siblings and myself on what she called "adventures." We would go hiking in state parks followed by ice cream and sometimes movies at the drive-in theater. She was like a second mother to me, for many of years our dysfunctional families were inseparable. After collecting myself, I rushed to my grandmother's home to be with my family, I also contacted my younger cousin because I was extremely worried about him.

He was an addict in active addiction. He professed to have been sober prior to my aunt's death, but also said he didn't think he could stay that way. Like most addicts including myself prior; we will say and do anything to try and take the focus off of ourselves when we are looked upon negatively, but we will con and manipulate anyone when we think it's to our advantage. There's an old saying, "You can't snow the snowman!" As soon as I picked my cousin up I knew that he was completely full of crap. However, he explained the nature of my aunt's suicide. She had been prescribed new medications and was drinking wine on top of them.

No one really knows the circumstances that triggered her to make that fateful decision. I'm not sure if anyone has ever received any real answers on why anyone would commit suicide. She wrote a note, then went out to the garage where her '67 Cutlass Supreme was. She took her cigarettes, a glass of wine, and the note, then turned the car on until she died of carbon monoxide poisoning. Some hours later her husband would discover her. This happened on a Sunday and ironically I remember leaving church on my motorcycle and sitting at a traffic light near her house. I remember hearing a small voice saying go visit her, but I did not listen to that voice as soon as the light changed I made my way toward home. This would've been around the same time that my aunt was carrying out her plan for suicide.

One valuable lesson I learned by the death of my aunt was to obey that small voice when it tells you to visit someone because you never know if you will see them again. As disheartening as it was I dropped my cousin off in the East Dayton slums after our conversation. I had to distance myself from him during his grief, he was trying to cover it up with drugs and alcohol. I could not afford to compromise my recovery. I didn't want any part of that rat race and needed to be strong for my family. He is still out there and in active addiction. I am not able to help him because he is not wanting to help himself nor does he have the capacity to be honest with himself or others. Now my mother and my Aunt had different Fathers. My aunt's dad was my number 2 grandpa. He had grown up in Kentucky and at an early age smoked non-filtered cigarettes for quite a number of years. He had quit smoking cold turkey nearly forty years prior to that late summer of 2016. It didn't stop him from paying the consequences with his health. He had COPD and had become frail. It wasn't long after the passing of my aunt and my mother would call me and said that it was urgent that I come to Grandma's. Grandpa had fallen trying to answer the door after what he thought someone was knocking at.

By the time I got to my grandmother's, he was incoherent and struggling to breathe. My grandmother had always kept a calm spirit about herself even after her daughter committed suicide. She contacted my grandpa's in home health agency. They came out and then had him admitted to Hospice. It only took a couple days before my grandpa passed away following shortly after his daughter.

Through the midst of all this pain God would reveal a blessing. It had been over one year since I had seen Layla. After thousands of dollars, numerous court visits, defending my integrity and almost becoming stripped of my rights. In the end, it was the power of prayer that changed Layla's mothers heart. She contacted me and said that she no longer wanted to fight or deprive Layla from seeing me. I was blown away just by how much my little girl had grown up in a year. I was also joyful to feel how much Layla loved and missed me. It was like she had become a different child; she was more affectionate and expressed loving words toward me. The Lord knew I needed that to soothe my hurting heart. I was also finally able to schedule some studio time for Risen from the Fall. We tracked and recorded the final song toward a five song EP. I felt a sense of accomplishment, all that was left was to have Noah mix and master everything. Just as soon as I got back from Nashville I was informed that my number 1 grandpa (my mom's dad) had been hospitalized at the VA. He had been suffering from some ongoing health issues for the last couple years but this time it would become fatal.

My mother and I planned on visiting him the day he passed away. We didn't make it to the hospital and it was probably better not having a last memory of him hurting. My grandpa was the man that laid the spiritual foundation for me to build my life on. The passing of him hurt extremely bad because I had such a profound love and respect for him. He took me to know who Jesus was at an early age, he also encouraged me and even when I was doing wrong he never chastised me but always would point me in the direction of Jesus. For that, I am forever grateful for his influence in my life. Whenever I was asked to speak at recovery functions, treatment centers or a church, I always included how special my grandpa was and quote Proverbs 22:6, "Train up a child in the way they should go, and when they are old they shall not depart from it." My grandpa did just that, for me. It took nearly twenty-five years, but I found my way back to Jesus.

Losing my grandpa created a moment of clarity. I knew that I had to realign my walk with Christ and also become more diligent in my recovery process. I reconnected with my sponsor who I had not spoken with in quite some time, I also started stepping up my meeting attendance. Making quiet time for prayer and reading the Bible. I also made sure that I was at Sons of Light Ministries every Sunday. I then again began to fill a sense of peace that surpasses all understanding. The one thing that I was unable to renew was my relationship with Melody.

We got into a bad argument just days before Christmas and I spent Christmas alone with Layla. I tried to maintain a smile for my little girl as she opened her gifts, but I knew that Melody and I had reached the end of the road. I confided my struggles to my Pastor at church. He was a biker and most everyone I attended church with was as well. He had joined a Christian Motorcycle Club called

Remnant Sons. He had asked me to consider getting involved with them months prior, because not only did he know how much I loved to ride, but he knew I had a heart for ministry. Most times he would mention it I would overlook it with minimal concern. However, after church one afternoon my Pastor invited me to Pittsburgh to attend a weekend seminar for Remnant Sons. He thought it would do me some good considering how emotionally exhausted I was.

Considering the passing away of my family members, the breakup of Melody and I, the frustrations with my band, and all the court battles regarding Layla. I accepted the invite. When we got to Pittsburgh, I knew I could expect a bunch of tattooed, bearded and leather wearing dudes. But what I did not expect was the presence and the power of the Holy Spirit. It was more than just a seminar, it was like church with the coolest people I had ever met that genuinely loved God. Following a service the Head Pastor invited anyone up who needed prayer.

I knew I needed prayer, but I sat silently in my chair until the pastor of my church said, "Dude, get up there and get your blessing!"

I approached the pulpit and when I was asked by the pastor how she could pray for me. I told her that I was hurting and grieving and wasn't feeling effective in my ministry. She anointed my head with oil and laid hands on me. She began praying boldly and I felt the presence of the Holy Spirit as if I was ascending on a jet plane. I began speaking in tongues which is something I have rarely done, simply because too much of myself stood in the way of allowing the Holy Spirit to intercede. I felt as though I was floating off the ground.

She commanded those lingering evil spirits to be gone from me, and plead the blood of Jesus over my life to renew my strength for His calling on my life. After she had finished praying I felt as though I was on a spiritual high. That very same night I made the decision that I wanted to become one of the Remnant Sons.

Later on that evening, a DJ would host karaoke and spin some music as we celebrated that weekend in the banquet hall. My Pastor insisted that I sing a song for everyone to hear. I chose to sing "Simple Man" by Lynard Skynard. I sang the song well enough that everyone stood and applauded; even the national president was impressed so much that he started calling me Hollywood. The name stuck with everyone in the club. That following Sunday morning I was rather bummed that we had to go back to Dayton, but I was extremely grateful for the family and the brothers I now had in Remnant Sons.

When I returned home I felt like all that oppression had been lifted from me. I had a new zeal for my walk with Christ, my recovery, and to become more productive in all aspects of my life. I sold my motorcycle and purchased a bigger Harley Davidson. I was even able to experience a very surreal moment by riding my bike to London Correctional Institution. I felt such an indescribable freedom by doing that. I also had a moment of clarity thanks to the Lord. I decided to put Risen from the Fall on hold and focus on finishing this book. I created a fund-raising campaign. At first it was discouraging, I had forty days to raise several thousand dollars for the editing and publishing expenses. The campaign would expire on my birthday, 4-13.

I continually prayed, "God if this be your will please allow it to be done." I had raised about half of my projected goal and then just minutes before the campaign would expire, a private donor would donate the remaining amount. It was the greatest birthday gift I have ever received. I was also still able to pursue my musical passions by leading worship at church and becoming re-acclimated with one of my former guitarists. He would join me at recovery functions where I would share my story followed by us playing some music acoustically. One of the most valuable lessons I have learned throughout my life is that when one door closes, God has already opened another door. Many of times I've had to walk through those open doors by blind faith. Learning patience, acceptance and how to persevere when things don't work out how I wanted them to.

That's what it means to become Risen from the Fall. I continually praise God for turning my mess into a message of hope. God's word is his promise, in Isaiah 61:3, it says, "To appoint unto them that mourn in Zion, to give unto them beauty for ashes, the oil of joy for mourning, the garment of praise for the spirit of heaviness; that they might be called trees of righteousness, the planting of the LORD, that he might be glorified.

Johnny Angel

Shelly Fabares sang a song in 1962 called "Johnny Angel." It's rather a silly love song, but I have fond memories of my mother singing it to me when I was younger. I used the name Johnny Angel on Facebook simply because of my childhood connection to it, and also the evangelical ministry I am called to. One of my favorite scriptural passages is out of Hebrews 13:2: "Do not forget to show hospitality to strangers, for by so doing some people have shown hospitality to angels without knowing it."

Late Saturday night on into early Sunday morning. I had been up working on this book in hopes of getting it finished. It was about 3:00 a.m., and I had hit a creative wall. I was sort of hungry so I decided to get into my truck and get a couple sandwiches from the fast food drive thru that was only a few blocks away. As I got into my truck, started it, and then made my way up the road I noticed a female walking up the road just under the overpass. I slowed the truck down a little bit and glanced over at her. She was stumbling and appeared to be drunk. She wore a skintight little black dress and had on a necklace that glistened by the moonlight. She was a rather attractive girl, and I instantly began to wonder, "Is this girl safe?" I drove past her and came to a red light.

As I was sitting there, I watched her in my rearview mirror struggling to walk. The Holy Spirit said to me, "Get out and make sure that girl is okay." My carnal mind said, "Dude, just go get your food and mind your own business." At first I chose to listen to the voice of my carnal mind. As I approached the restaurant I then heard the voice of the Holy Spirit again, but this time it was loud saying, "Turn around, go get that girl!" So I did just that, I made a U-turn in the road, turned back at the light, and there she was. She could barely walk, she was crying and I was worried that she had been beaten up. As I pulled up to her and then stopped, without hesitation she approached my truck opened the door and began pleading for me to give her a ride. She was very hysterical so I interrupted her and said, "Are you ok?" "What Happened?" She informed me that someone had taken her car. She climbed inside the truck and began telling me that she was an exotic dancer that had too much to drink so the management at the club took her car keys. I told her that was a blessing because she was wasted drunk. She then asked me if I was going to give her a ride, and I asked her where she needed to go. She told me downtown, and that she would give me twenty dollars if I did. I didn't want her money and I told her that. I then told her I can give you a ride but I will not take you inside the downtown area.

My birthday had just passed and I hadn't renewed my tags so I was in fear of getting pulled over and getting a ticket. Downtown was always full of cops. So we made our way down the road. I began telling her that what she was doing by trying to walk downtown which was over five miles away was rather dangerous. I told her that she got lucky by having a good guy stop. I warned her that she could of been picked up by some creep, kidnapped, drugged and then sold into sex trafficking. What I was saying to her seemed to go in one ear and out the other. So I said, "Look, I'm going to get real honest with you, you could have died out here tonight!" I proceeded to tell her the story of my little sister prior to her arrest and then losing her life. Suddenly the young girl I had picked up began to listen. She asked, "How old was she, when she died?" My reply was twenty years old. I then asked her how old she was. There was a long pause, followed by her response, and she said, "I am twenty years old."

There was a moment of silence, and in that silence I believe she was thinking really hard. What was going on inside that mind of hers, I had no idea. I'm not even sure that she could fully comprehend the seriousness of what I tried to share with her. Ultimately her fate would be left in God's hands. But that night God saw it fit to disguise me as an angel and keep her safe. I pulled up to the edge of downtown to drop her off, she began fumbling around in her purse looking for twenty dollars to give me. I insisted that I did not need her money. She didn't even have any money. Just a bag full of skimpy outfits and thong underwear. It broke my heart to think about what could've happened to her. It also made me miss my sister; the big brother in me was doing for this young lady, what I could no longer do for my sister. I had a moment of clarity and decided to take the risk of driving to whatever apartment she was going to downtown. I couldn't have lived with the guilt if I dropped her off just blocks away and something happened to her. I did only what any respectable father or brother would do for a twenty-year-old girl. By the grace of God, I did not see one cop during that twenty-minute drive. I pulled up to a traffic light where a condo complex was just on the right.

She said, "You can let me out here." She got out of my truck and made her way toward the sidewalk, stumbling and tripping over the curb. She skinned both of her knees and got back up, laughing. It was no laughing matter to me because I knew just how dangerous the party lifestyle was. She thanked me for the ride, then made her way toward the porch of one of the buildings. She went inside, so I sat for about five or ten minutes to see if she would come back out. I wanted to make sure that someone was there to receive her. I have no idea who that person was, but I didn't want that young lady walking around downtown Dayton at three thirty in the morning. She didn't come back out, so I drove away and got on the highway headed toward home.

I don't consider it ironic that this happened on a Sunday just before putting the finishing touches on *87 Sundays*. God always finds a way of reminding me of who I am, where I have come from, and where I should be going. Doors open, and doors close; people come, and people go. The one thing that is constant is God, recovery, and to carry the message of hope to those who still suffer. No matter what hour or day, they will receive the message of *87 Sundays*.

About the Author

J ohnny G. Baxter, a.k.a Johnny Angel, is a Christ follower and in long-term recovery from all mood- and mind-altering substances. His clean date is October 22, 2010. He is an advocate for recovery and speaks at treatment centers, jails, prisons, churches, and recovery-based rallies in and around his hometown of Dayton, Ohio. Dayton has become no. 1 in the entire nation for heroin/opioid–related overdoses and deaths. Johnny is also a musician in the band known as Risen from the Fall. Johnny enjoys spending time with his daughter, Layla, riding his motorcycle with his brothers in the Remnant Sons Motorcycle Club, and working out in the gym. Johnny values his walk with Christ first and foremost. He is a member of Sons of Light Ministries located in Dayton and realizes that it was God's touch of healing grace that allowed him to experience true freedom and to carry the message of *87 Sundays*.

CPSIA information can be obtained
at www.ICGtesting.com
Printed in the USA
LVOW08s1621300118
564584LV00001B/162/P